Gun Control

GUN CONTROL

*Public Safety
and the Right
to Bear Arms*

Ted Gottfried

*The Millbrook Press
Brookfield, Connecticut*

Issue and Debate

Photographs courtesy of Woodfin Camp & Associated, Inc.: pp. 15, 19, 40, 89 (Alon Reininger), 33 (Dan Budnik), 68 (J. B. Diederich); Bettmann Archive: pp. 26, 31, 61; AP/Wide World Photos: pp. 39, 49, 52, 71, 84, 93; Black Star (Mitch Kezan): p.56; UPI/Bettmann: pp. 63, 73; Reuters/Bettmann: p. 80.

Library of Congress Cataloging-in-Publication Data

Gottfried, Ted.
Gun control : public safety and the right to bear arms / by Ted Gottfried.
p.   cm.—(Issue and debate)
Includes bibliographical references and index.
Summary: Presents arguments for and against the licensing and control of firearms in the United States, examining the historical role of guns, the constitutionality of restricting gun ownership, past and current legislation, and proposals for new restrictions.
ISBN 1-56294-342-1 (lib. bdg.)
1. Gun control—United States—Juvenile literature.   [1. Gun control.]   I. Title.   II. Series.
HV7436.G66   1993
363.3'3'0973—dc20   92-32775   CIP   AC

Published by The Millbrook Press
2 Old New Milford Road, Brookfield, Connecticut 06804

For Kyle Gutierrez
With Peace and Love

Books by Ted Gottfried

Enrico Fermi: The Father of the Atom Bomb

The Illustrated Treasury of Famous Movie Lines

Clemenceau (a biography)

Qaddafi (a biography)

The House of Diamond (a novel)

Acknowledgments

I want to thank Odile Stern of Handgun Control, Richard Aborn and Caroline Abdulah of the Center for Prevention of Handgun Violence, Karen Mehall of the National Rifle Association, and staff members of the New York Public Library and of the Queensboro Public Library for their help in researching material for this book. I would also like to acknowledge help, guidance, and the sharing of research material by the award-winning author of young adult books Janet Bode. I am grateful for the help and support of my agent Kathy Preminger and of my editor, Elaine Pascoe. Last, but not least, thanks to my wife, Harriet Gottfried, who—as always—read and critiqued this book.

All contributed, but any shortcomings in the work are mine alone.

Ted Gottfried

Contents

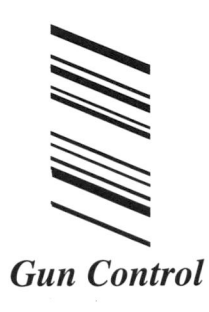

Gun Control

Introduction

There are presently in excess of 200 million guns in the United States, according to the Bureau of Alcohol, Tobacco and Firearms. Each year this number grows by 4 to 5 million. There are 60 to 65 million legal owners of one or more guns. There is a firearm on the premises of more than half the households in America. Most of them keep guns for protection. The others keep them for hunting, target shooting, collecting, and similar pursuits.

In recent years nearly 35,000 people have been killed annually by guns in the United States. These deaths include 15,000 murders, 18,000 suicides, and 1,500 accidents. The Centers for Disease Control's National Center for Health Statistics reports that one out of every ten American youngsters who die is killed with a gun. In the fifteen- to nineteen- year-old age group, the figures are higher. Eighteen percent of white males who die and 48 percent of African-American males who die are victims of firearms. This is a 107 percent increase for all males in this age group since 1984.

Young people are members of families that own guns. Young people are victims of guns. Obviously, the question of just what restrictions, if any, should be placed on these firearms is as much a matter of concern to them as to their elders. Still, it is to their elders, the leaders among them at least, that they must look for guidance—if not, perhaps, for answers.

America's leaders disagree about gun control. Senator Edward Kennedy of Massachusetts, whose two brothers—one a U.S. president, the other a candidate for the presidency—were both killed by assassins wielding firearms, has said: "Our nation is armed to the teeth at home. Our society is becoming an arsenal of criminal anarchy. . . . We must say again and again that . . . crime control means gun control."

President Ronald Reagan, himself the victim of an assassin's pistol, had a different opinion. "It's a nasty truth, but those who seek to inflict harm are not fazed by gun-control laws. . . . Guns don't make criminals; hardcore criminals use guns. . . . We will never disarm any American who seeks to protect his or her family from fear and harm."

In later years President Reagan modified his position. President George Bush, a "life member" of the National Rifle Association, which opposes most gun control legislation, supported some controls and opposed most. His Democratic opponent in the 1992 election, Arkansas Governor Bill Clinton, supported pro-control legislation pending in Congress as well as a ban on assault weapons. Clinton won the election, making some type of federal legislation more likely. Still, with half their constituents owning firearms, many legislators were not sure the American people want gun control.

Some certainly do not. Prior to the April 1992 riots in Los Angeles, legal gun sales were booming in that city.

A collection of guns confiscated by police is evidence of the problems posed by the easy availability of firearms in the United States.

Women in particular were buying guns and going to ranges to learn how to shoot. In those areas of the inner city where youth gangs were the rule, male teenagers routinely carried illegal guns as a matter of survival on mean streets and in violent schools.

Los Angeles authorities estimate that some two thousand firearms, many of them heavy duty semiautomatic weapons, were stolen from pawn shops and gun shops during the rioting. In the aftermath, police sweeps tried to recover them. But with the street prices of the guns reduced for quick cash, most were quickly distributed.

People in L.A.'s poor neighborhoods were terrified at the prospect of still more guns on the street in addition to those already there. Those in other L.A. areas reacted quite differently. After the riots, legal gun sales outside the inner city climbed to record highs. This was true across the nation. People who already had guns traded them in for more lethal weapons with more effective firepower. Middle-class and upper-class women began to learn to shoot rifles and automatic weapons as well as pistols. Some citizens huddle in terror; others take up arms.

These attitudes mirror both sides of the gun control question. Some people fear that the more guns there are the more violence will result. Others feel that if the criminals have guns, then citizens, too, must be armed to protect themselves.

Such gut-level responses are simple. The questions to which they give rise, however, are not. These are the issues we will look at in the chapters that follow.

They Each
Had a Gun

Although Hannah LaMarca and Arthur Strang* both lived in the same middle-class midwestern suburb, they did not know each other. It was by chance that they acquired their handguns on the same day. But it was something more than chance that pushed them into getting their firearms.

Arthur Strang had become alarmed by a rash of robberies on his block. In one case a neighbor was pistol-whipped by two of the burglars. In another, a watchdog, a family pet, was killed. Arthur Strang thought about it and decided he and his wife and two children needed protection. He applied for a gun license, and when it came through he bought a .38 caliber Smith & Wesson revolver.

Hannah LaMarca was a single woman who shared an apartment in a two-family house with two other women.

* Hannah LaMarca and Arthur Strang are composites of case histories compiled by the National Rifle Association in *The Armed Citizen* (1989), and of examples cited by the Center to Prevent Handgun Violence, Handgun Control Inc., and various law enforcement agencies.

One night, after dinner and a movie with an office friend, Hannah was returning home alone when a man emerged from the shadows of the tree-lined street on which she lived and demanded that she hand over her pocketbook. He was a small man and didn't seem to be armed, and so she hesitated. Should she scream, run, or do what he demanded?

She never had a chance to decide. She never saw what hit her. When she regained consciousness a while later in the arms of the neighbor who found her, Hannah's cheekbone was shattered and her jaw fractured. From the bruise marks it was later determined that she had been struck three times by brass knuckles. Her pocketbook, and the small amount of money in it, was gone.

"It wasn't just the money," Hannah said. "Or even being beaten up. I'd been violated in a much worse way. You see, I'd never given much thought to my safety. Now I would never feel safe again."

She applied for a license to carry a small pistol, a so-called "lady's revolver," which fit into her handbag. Then she joined a gun club and went through an intensive course on target shooting. She learned to hit what she aimed at from various distances and under pressure.

Hannah LaMarca's ownership of a firearm was a reaction to being a victim. Arthur Strang's purchase of a revolver was his response to the fear of becoming one. Perhaps his fear was less immediate, and that is why, once he had the gun, he never even fired it.

He showed it to his wife and to their children. Arthur and Charlotte Strang had two children—Michelle, age fourteen, and Neil, who was eleven. After he showed it to them, Arthur put the .38 in a drawer of the night table beside his bed, where it would be handy if needed to repel an intruder. Everybody in the family knew where the gun was kept in case it was ever needed for protection.

Hoping to defend themselves from crime, growing numbers of people have purchased handguns and learned to use them in classes such as this.

The situation that Arthur Strang feared never occurred. A similar situation, however, did present itself to Hannah LaMarca. She was home alone one night, dozing over a book she'd been reading in bed, when she heard noises coming from the bedroom of one of her housemates. Hannah took out her pistol and went to investigate.

A man she had never seen before was coming through the window as she opened the door to the bedroom. He landed on his feet and lurched forward. Hannah LaMarca fired three times. All three bullets hit the intruder in the chest, killing him.

Some weeks later, Arthur Strang's eleven-year-old son Neil told his friend Bruce Kammerer about the .38 his father kept in the night table. Bruce was interested and asked to see it. Neil took Bruce up to his parents' bedroom and started to remove the pistol from the drawer.

"Is it loaded?" Bruce Kammerer asked.

Before Neil could answer that he wasn't sure, the gun slipped from his hand, hit the baseboard and the floor simultaneously, and fired. The bullet struck Bruce Kammerer in the side of the skull. He died instantly.

Neil Strang, like Hannah LaMarca, had killed a fellow human being with a firearm. He had done so accidentally, she deliberately. A gun had slain a child. A gun had stopped a crime. Two people were dead: an innocent boy, and a criminal who, as it turned out, had a prior record of burglary arrests. As different as the circumstances were, each of these cases provokes opposite reactions from those who are for gun control and those who are against it.

In Hannah LaMarca's case, those who think citizens should arm themselves are satisfied that their point has been proven. A woman successfully protected her property and herself against a potentially dangerous criminal. A victim struck back. There is one less lawbreaker to threaten society, and we are all the better for it. The weapon Hannah LaMarca used is a tool that, to some small extent, has shaped a more decent and law-abiding world for all of us. The gun is an instrument to ensure our quality of life.

With equally strong conviction, gun-control advocates view the tragic shooting of eleven-year-old Bruce Kammerer as grim proof of the rightness of their position. Some (but not all) believe that Arthur Strang should never have had a gun in his home in the first place. There were other measures he could have taken to protect his property and his family. He could have installed safety locks and an alarm system. He could have gotten a watchdog. (Police interviews reveal that most professional thieves will not target a home where a watchdog is present.) They say the gun posed more of a threat to Arthur Strang and his family than to any robber. (They cite cases in which the sight of a gun in the hands of a homeowner provoked an armed intruder to shoot first.) Strang's gun was one more addition to the mounting violence of our world, they conclude, and Bruce Kammerer's death demonstrates the truth of that judgment.

They also challenge the conclusions drawn by their opponents regarding Hannah LaMarca's slaying of the housebreaker. If robbery is not legally punishable by a death sentence, then what right does a private citizen have to shoot and kill a burglar? they ask. Was Hannah LaMarca's fear—stemming from her previous experience—a justification? Was her fear realistic? Was her life in danger or were only her possessions at risk?

Despite his previous criminal record, the second-story man was unarmed. Nor had he been armed when committing the crimes for which he had previously been arrested. Just how much force is justified—legally or morally—to protect property? Is killing an appropriate response? If lethal punishment is to be the answer to every crime, gun-control advocates insist, then the climate of violence that results will undermine the moral fiber of our society.

But it is that very moral fiber that concerns those who champion a citizen's right to be armed. In their view, if criminals have guns and decent people do not, then that aspect of society we call "civilized" will surely be destroyed. To fight for what is right is an individual obligation, and to be armed is to see to it that one is at least on equal terms with those criminal elements we all must oppose.

Yes, they concede, the shooting of eleven-year-old Bruce Kammerer was a tragedy. Terrible accidents do happen to children. But, they remind us, most such accidents do not involve firearms. The right to self-protection cannot be set aside because there are unfortunate incidents. More children by far die by fire than are slain by guns, but we do not license or limit the sale of matches.

Arthur Strang should not be criticized for having bought a gun, they say, but rather for treating it negligently. He had an obligation to familiarize himself with its use. He had an obligation to see that it was properly secured where neither children nor interlopers could get at it. Above all, he had an obligation to see that it was not loaded.

Firearms advocates like to stress the need for such safety precautions. But their demand that a gun be treated with respect does not answer the concerns of their opponents, who find inconsistencies in the position.

If a gun is secured out of the reach of others, they point out, then it will not be easily accessible when needed. If it is not loaded, then of what use is it as protection? Is the housebreaker going to stand by idly while the homeowner puts bullets in the chambers? Yes, if there are to be guns, then safety precautions are crucial.

But if observing them cancels out the purpose of the firearm, then why have it in the first place?

Back and forth the argument goes. A gun stopped a crime; a gun killed a child. Guns are protection. Guns are dangerous.

Who is right?

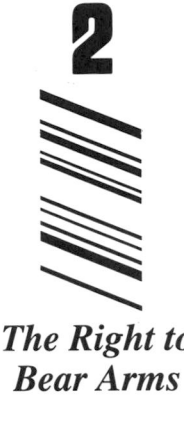

The Right to
Bear Arms

In the American Revolution, "victory over the British army was made possible by the existence of an already-armed people," points out Howard Zinn in *A People's History of the United States*. "Just about every male had a gun and could shoot," he adds. That historian Zinn is also a leading advocate of nonviolence tells us how complex the question of gun ownership can be.

The reason the American colonists were armed was that they lived under English common law. Since 1689 all Englishmen, including those in the colonies, had enjoyed certain privileges under the English Bill of Rights. There were thirteen of these rights, and the seventh guaranteed "that the subjects . . . may have Arms for their Defence suitable to their Condition and as allowed by Law." This meant that every Englishman (but not customarily every woman) could keep weapons to protect himself and to protect his country, if necessary.

When the American Revolution began, one of the first proposals by the British Colonial Office for dealing with it was that "the Militia Laws should be repealed and

*Minutemen of the Revolutionary
War era gathered on village greens
to drill with their weapons.*

. . . the Arms of all the People should be taken away." But the British couldn't enforce that. The armed colonists would not surrender their muskets. Instead they fought for their independence and won it.

The Second Amendment. After the new nation was formed, the laws that still govern it were hammered out at a constitutional convention. But after the U.S. Constitution was ratified, there was concern that certain basic rights had not been covered. The citizens had not forgotten the role that weapons played in the recent struggle. It was evident that the right to bear arms was one of those basic rights.

Concern over omissions in the Constitution led to the adoption of the first ten amendments, known as the Bill of Rights. All ten were added at the same time in a package meant to protect those freedoms not addressed in the original document. They were written by James Madison, later elected fourth president of the United States, and modified and reworded by the first U.S. Congress. The Bill of Rights was adopted in 1791. Over the years, each of its ten amendments has been interpreted and reinterpreted as times and attitudes and circumstances have changed. An effort has always been made to preserve the original meaning while adapting the application to modern conditions. This has never been easy, and perhaps particularly hard in the case of the Second Amendment. It is only twenty-seven words long:

> *A well-regulated militia being necessary to the security of a free state, the right of the people to keep and bear Arms shall not be infringed.*

When it was adopted, the Second Amendment was really only approving the existing situation. The United States was still mainly a rural country, and most citizens still hunted for at least some of their food, and so of course they were armed. In many areas, conflicts with Native Americans were ongoing, and muskets were considered necessary to the defense of home and family. By the time the War of 1812 started, the English were met not just by military force but by an armed citizenry.

As the years passed, however, the use of guns to settle personal disputes and to commit crimes aroused concern at the local level. In 1846 in Georgia, a law was passed prohibiting possession of the "breast pistol"—the sort of firearm most often used in illegal duels and in holdups (it was lightweight and relatively easy to conceal). But the Georgia courts struck down the law, declaring that the Second Amendment prohibition against infringing on the right of the people to bear arms applied to the state as well as the federal government and insisting that there was not "anything in its terms which restricts its meaning."

The Georgia court spelled out the strict interpretation of the Second Amendment which those most strongly against gun control still insist on today. Neither federal, state, nor local government may pass a law interfering with the citizen's right to be armed. This is not the position of everyone who opposes gun control, but it is the constitutional interpretation on which their opposition rests.

New Interpretations. It was not until 1876 that this interpretation was challenged in the U.S. Supreme Court, in a case known as *United States* v. *Cruikshank*. The white defendants in the case had been convicted of depriving African-American citizens of their constitutional rights as guaranteed by the Civil Rights Act of 1870. This included the right to bear arms as ensured by the Second Amendment. The defendants had conspired to prevent the African-Americans from assembling while carrying guns. They had also confiscated their weapons.

The Supreme Court decided that bearing arms "is not a right granted by the Constitution. . . . The Second Amendment declares that it shall not be infringed; but this . . . means no more than that it shall not be infringed by Congress."

Those who favor gun control take this to mean that state and local governments are free to regulate firearms in any way they see fit. And they go further. They say that the *Cruikshank* decision interprets the Second Amendment to mean that *federal* regulation and licensing of guns do not "infringe" on the right to bear arms.

A parallel example would be that every adult person may have the right to own a car, but each person must be licensed to drive and is subject to rules and regulations for the common good. The basic right is not "infringed" by common-sense restrictions. It is merely limited for the good of all.

Opponents of gun control disagree. Richard Gardiner, an attorney specializing in constitutional interpretation who is legislative counsel for the National Rifle Association's Institute for Legislative Action, insists that in *Cruikshank*, "the Court plainly recognized that the right of the people to keep and bear arms was a fundamental right which existed prior to the Constitution . . ." The NRA also sees *Cruikshank* as absolutely forbidding *federal* legislation restricting ownership of guns in any way.

Ten years after *Cruikshank*, in 1886, the case of *Presser* v. *Illinois* resulted in another Supreme Court decision that is still interpreted differently by supporters and opponents of gun control. Four hundred armed men led by Presser marched through Chicago. The State of Illinois convicted Presser of assembling and parading them without a license. The Supreme Court upheld the conviction.

The decision was based on narrow grounds having to do with the meaning of the Second Amendment's reference to "a well-regulated militia." The Court pointed out that Presser "was not a member of the organized volunteer militia of the State of Illinois . . . or of any organization under the militia law of the United States." In other words, the Court was saying that Presser as an individual had no constitutional right to arm and organize others to arm in defiance of state licensing regulations. Some of those who want to restrict gun ownership read this decision to mean that Presser (or any other individual) only had the constitutional right to bear arms as a member of an authorized government militia.

Those against gun control read *Presser* differently. They quote a different section of the decision: "All citizens capable of bearing arms constitute the . . . reserve militia of the United States . . . The States cannot . . . prohibit the people from keeping and bearing arms, so as to . . . disable the people from performing their duty to the general government." They say this means that states and local communities can't pass laws that interfere with citizens arming themselves to protect their country.

Examining the Amendment. In the hundred years since *Presser*, Supreme Court decisions have confirmed more and more strongly the authority of states and communities to regulate gun sales, ownership, and use. There has never been a successful challenge to the constitutionality of the Federal Gun Control Act of 1968, which forbids crossing a state line to buy a handgun. However, the legal arguments surrounding each new proposal restricting guns always come back to the meaning of the Second Amendment.

As we have seen, the amendment's first phrase—"a well-regulated militia"—can be interpreted in opposing ways. So too can the four other phrases that make up the twenty-seven words of the Second Amendment.

What exactly is "necessary for the security of a free state"? No *individual* can serve this purpose by himself or

Concern about firearms has a long history in the United States, as seen in this cartoon from the late 1800s.

herself, according to those who favor gun control. National security is a *collective* obligation, and only the government can arm and organize individuals to use guns to defend a free state. The phrase was never intended to mean that any militiaman should operate independent of authority. That authority, they say, includes the regulation of firearms.

Not so, insists the other side. The right to bear arms belongs to the individual because it is part of the right to self-defense recognized by English and American common law. If not for this, the frontiers of America might never have been extended. Individuals forming themselves into groups for self-defense—regardless of official permission—are necessary to maintain a civilized society. During the Cold War this right was cited as necessary to repel a possible invasion. Today it is insisted upon by many survivalist groups.

"The right of the people" is the third phrase at issue. Gun-control advocates say it refers to "the people" collectively, as represented by their elected officials, and not to individuals acting on their own. The people may arm according to law; the individual may not arm in defiance of it.

But firearms devotees translate the grammar differently. They see "the people" as referring to each of us. They say the "right" referred to—gun ownership—is reserved for each person.

The right that "people" have, according to the Second Amendment, is "to keep and bear arms." Does that really mean gun ownership and the carrying of a gun on one's person? Not according to gun-control lobbyists, who say that while a militia may "bear" arms, the individual citizen "carries" a gun. The arms that the militia "keep" are really not theirs, rather government property entrusted

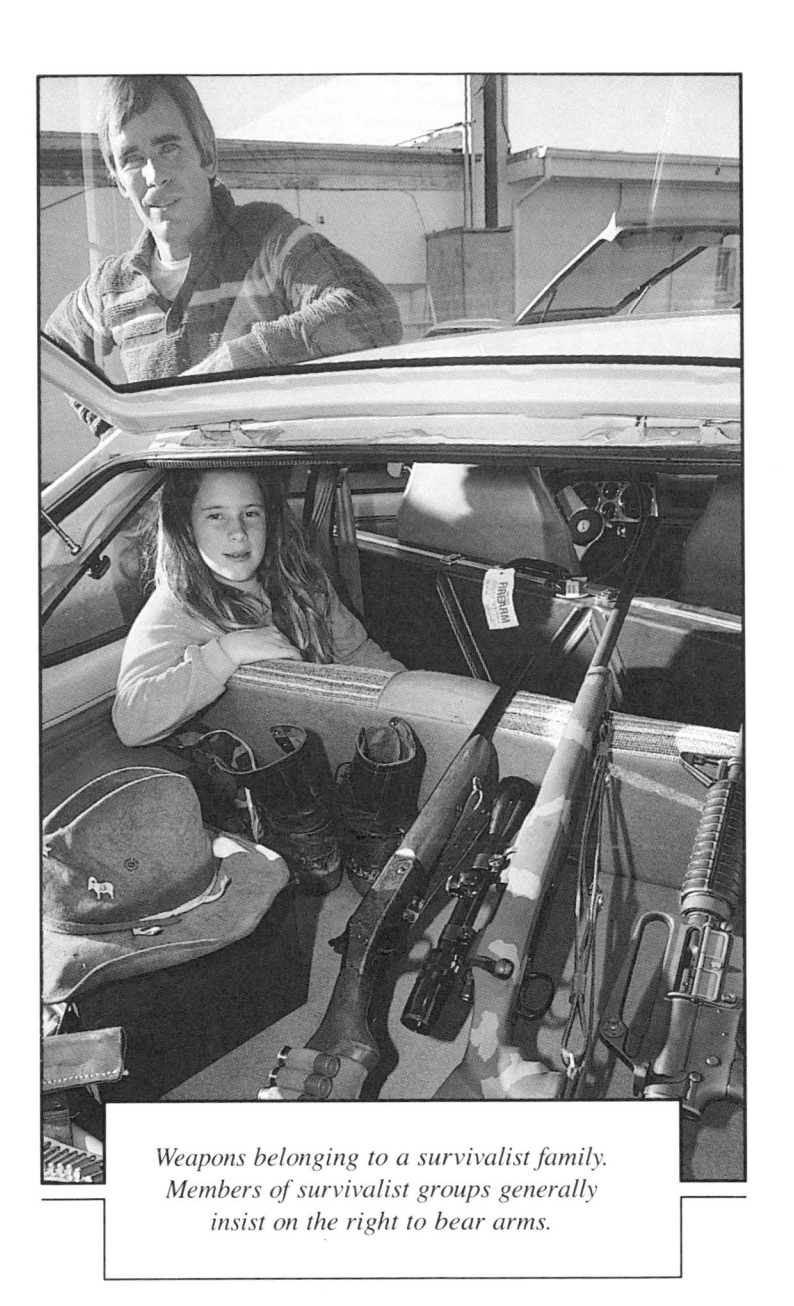

Weapons belonging to a survivalist family.
Members of survivalist groups generally
insist on the right to bear arms.

to them. An individual, therefore, has no Second Amendment right to own a gun, only perhaps to keep one during his period of service to the militia.

Going further, they define "arms" as weapons issued by the militia and specifically not guns used for hunting, target-shooting, or even self-protection. Backing this up is the 1939 Supreme Court decision in *United States* v. *Miller*, in which a shotgun with a barrel less than 18 inches (46 centimeters) long was confirmed as subject to federal regulation because it would not be used by "a well-regulated militia."

Gun advocates fume at such reasoning. They read "to keep and bear arms" as a clear statement of their right to own any kind of firearm. The Second Amendment does not define "arms," and they see no reason why the Supreme Court should narrow the commonly accepted dictionary definition. As to differences between "bear" and "carry," and "keep" and "own," they dismiss them as "desperate hair-splitting" on the part of the gun-control lobby.

The final phrase is "shall not be infringed." One side takes it literally as an absolute prohibition against gun control. The other side looks at the word "infringed" in the context of "a well-regulated militia" and does not believe control over individual gun owners falls within its application.

Similarly, interpretations of the Second Amendment during the last few years have led to diametrically opposite legislation. Two small communities—Morton Grove, Illinois, and Kennesaw, Georgia—passed very different gun laws. The Morton Grove law forbade the ownership of any and all handguns. The Kennesaw statute required every able-bodied man in Kennesaw to own a gun that could be used for the common defense of the community. Both laws are being challenged in the courts.

If these cases eventually reach the U.S. Supreme Court, they may be affected by a decision by that body in the case of *United States* v. *Verdugo-Urquidez*. Writing the majority opinion in that case on February 28, 1990, Chief Justice William Rehnquist indicated that rights guaranteed by the Constitution are *individual* rights. He noted that the Second Amendment was not alone in referring to "people" rather than "persons" when defining the rights of the individual. He cited the Preamble and the Fourth, Ninth, and Tenth Amendments of the Constitution as referring to "a class of persons who are part of a national community" who hold individual rights in common. In this view, the right of the "people" to keep and bear arms refers to each one of the people individually.

The latest focus of the Second Amendment battle is the Brady Bill, which would establish a national standard for buying a handgun. The bill is named for former president Ronald Reagan's press secretary, James Brady, who was permanently disabled by a bullet fired by a man attempting to assassinate the president in 1981. It would require a week-long waiting period before the granting of an application to buy a gun, to allow time for background checks on gun purchasers by local law enforcement agencies.

The Second Amendment played a large part in the Congressional debate over this bill. Those who opposed it brought in the Constitutional issue of "prior restraint," claiming that the bill violated the "assumption of innocence," which is the foundation of our legal system. The Brady Bill, they said, was based on an assumption of guilt that made each potential gun buyer prove his or her blamelessness before being allowed to make the purchase. Since the Second Amendment confirmed the *right* to have a gun, that right could not be taken away in advance of any wrongdoing.

In 1991 and again in 1992, the Brady Bill failed to pass, individually or as part of a larger crime bill with many controversial provisions. Ultimately its fate may depend on Second Amendment arguments. After President Clinton took office in 1993, passage of some version of the bill seemed more likely. But even if the Brady Bill is passed and signed into law, the Supreme Court might still strike it down on Second Amendment grounds.

And so the question remains: Does the Second Amendment guarantee a precious right? Or is it a roadblock to a less violent society?

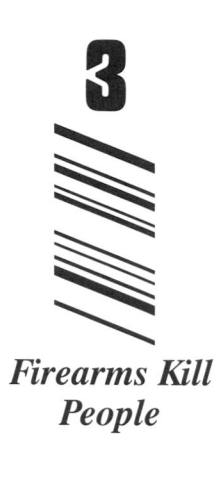

3

Firearms Kill People

To those who campaign for stricter gun-control laws, each day's headlines provide examples to bolster their position. In big cities, suburbs, and rural areas alike, more and more innocent people are being maimed or killed by bullets. These bullets are fired from guns that often were bought legally and are too easily resold in areas where such sales are not legal.

Restrictions on firearms in some communities are undermined by the ease with which they can be bought in less restrictive areas and transported. For instance, anti-gun crusaders point out, there is regular traffic between midwestern cities where guns are sold legally and Chicago, which has laws against gun sales. The illegal flow of guns into the city has grown beyond the ability of police to control it. According to the *New York Times* of March 11, 1992, "In one sad neighborhood here, where funerals for young men and boys are now commonplace, people say the Gun Man drives through the streets selling pistols from the back of a light-blue van."

Guns and Youth. In New York City, which also has gun laws it can't enforce because of guns pouring in from Virginia and other states, a particularly shocking incident pointed up how bad the problem has become. On February 27, 1992, Mayor David Dinkins was scheduled to speak at Thomas Jefferson High School in the city's borough of Brooklyn. Fifteen uniformed policemen were on the school premises. However, the metal detector designed to keep firearms out of the school was not in operation. A fifteen-year-old boy walked past the police and up to two other male students, ages sixteen and seventeen. He pulled out a .38 caliber Smith & Wesson revolver and shot the older youths, killing both.

Later that same day, another sixteen-year-old boy, discussing the killings with a friend over the phone, boasted that even as they talked he was playing Russian roulette. The statement was followed by the sound of a gunshot. The victim was rushed to the hospital in critical condition, a bullet lodged in his brain. He later died.

These were only the latest in a series of incidents involving guns in Thomas Jefferson High School. Indeed, guns have long been a major problem in all the city schools, as well as in schools in other urban (and many suburban) areas across the country. Nearly 8.7 million youngsters have access to handguns, reports the National School Safety Center. According to the Committee on Trauma of the American Academy of Pediatrics, during the late 1980s one out of every twenty-five children treated at United States pediatric facilities was treated for gunshot wounds. To the Center to Prevent Handgun Violence, the direct relationship between these figures adds up to a demand for action.

The Center cites other related reports: Gun murders of people nineteen years old and younger have increased by 97 percent since 1984, according to two studies based

A guard with a metal detector checks the possessions of a student at Thomas Jefferson High School in Brooklyn, New York, following the 1992 shooting death of two youths there.

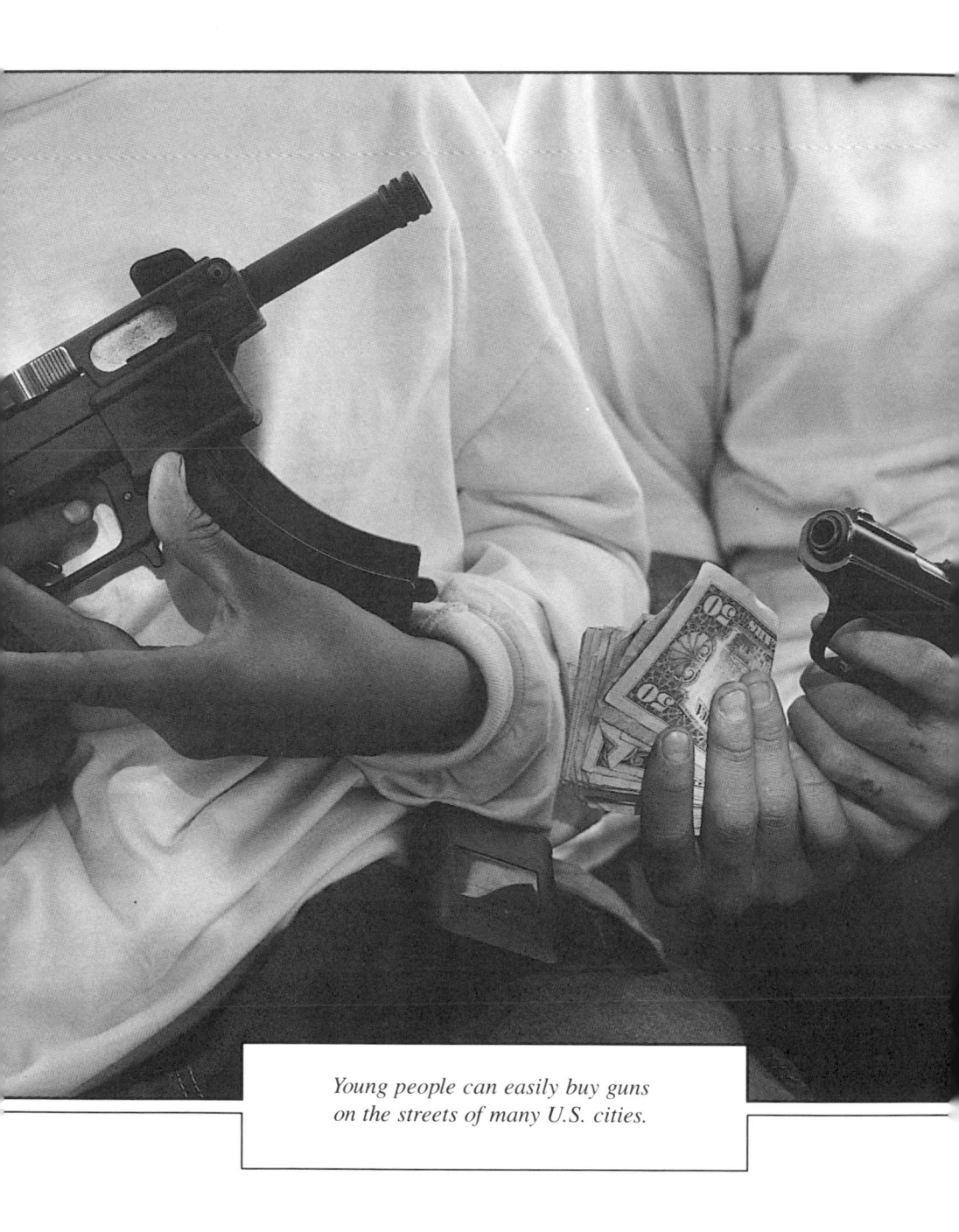

*Young people can easily buy guns
on the streets of many U.S. cities.*

on data published by the F.B.I. in its annual *Uniform Crime Report*. The figures for 1989 show that three out of five young people murdered in America were killed with guns.

This carnage strikes hardest at the youth of the inner cities, where poverty is greatest. It is in poor neighborhoods that illegal guns are most easily available. The road from hardship to gunplay is well traveled.

At the root of poverty is lack of opportunity, which breeds hopelessness. Many people who are hopeless turn to liquor and to drugs. Others seek opportunity outside the law by peddling those drugs. Too frequently, ambitious underprivileged youngsters take this route.

But competition is fierce among drug peddlers. Established pushers don't hesitate to use guns to keep control of their turf. Young newcomers view fighting back with guns as a matter of survival. "An eye for an eye!" says the sixteen-year-old Mexican-American leader of a youth gang that deals drugs in Phoenix, Arizona. "That way all of our young people will end up blind," is the answer from a Boston, Massachusetts, youth counselor who believes that the first step in dealing with such problems should be passing the kind of strong federal legislation that will get the guns off the streets.

Lesser measures can't work, say those who favor strict gun control. There are 125 youth gangs with up to 20,000 members in Chicago alone. They accounted for 924 homicide victims in 1991, 70 percent of whom died from gunshot wounds. Yet the sale of handguns has been illegal in Chicago for almost ten years.

Dealers like the Gun Man in the blue van regularly beat the law. The *New York Times* reports that "crooked gun dealers, gunrunners who bring in weapons bought in the suburbs or out of state, brigades of burglars and flea-market traders who are happy to sell to any customer" keep the guns flowing to Chicago youth gangs. In February 1992, the Chicago police closed down an illegal gun store operating across the street from an elementary school.

A month later an eight-year-old Chicago boy brought a gun from his home to school and shot a girl in his third-grade class in the back. She was rushed to the hospital in serious condition. The local police precinct commander described her as "just another innocent victim."

Innocent Victims. The number of innocent bystanders who become victims increases as guns become more and more easily available, say the anti-gun forces. The heartbreak of such incidents was pointed up in early 1992 when a Bronx, New York, schoolteacher was caught in a crossfire between two gunmen while seated at the wheel of her car, waiting for a traffic light to change. The teacher had taught children in the area for over twenty years. She was much loved and respected by her students for her mostly successful efforts to steer them away from violence. Now she became the victim of senseless violence. She died of her wounds.

That guns so often kill people who themselves have nothing to do with firearms is one reason major organizations have lined up on the side of federal gun control. They include the American Medical Association, the American Bar Association, the League of Women Voters, the National Education Association, the National League of Cities, and the U.S. Conference of Mayors. All have allied themselves with such gun-control lobbying organizations as the Coalition to Stop Gun Violence and Handgun Control, Inc.

Many major U.S. police associations support some version of federal gun control. Law enforcement officers are frequent victims of the guns on the streets. They often confront firepower superior to their own. In 1989 the Police Executive Research Forum passed a resolution announcing that it "has long supported sensible firearms laws" and "believes that reasonable regulation of firearms can reduce the carnage inflicted with these weapons."

The carnage is not confined to cities. Increasingly, the spread of crime to the suburbs has brought guns and bloodshed in its wake. The guns, often purchased to protect home, family, and property, frequently become the instruments of tragedy.

Nor do the guns always do what they were bought to do. They often bring on the very result they are meant to prevent. One police chief, quoted in the *Washington Post*, put it this way: "When an attacker sees a victim lift and aim a handgun . . . he will most assuredly use his own weapon quickly. The police experience is that the consequences of such confrontations are more serious than if the victim had no weapon."

A firearm on the premises is viewed by many gun-control proponents as an accident waiting to happen. In New Jersey the pistol bought by one man to protect his property was found by his three-year-old grandson. The little boy took it from the drawer, inadvertently pulled the trigger, and killed himself. Under a New Jersey law which makes a gun's owner responsible for keeping the weapon away from minors, the grandfather faced criminal charges.

In Trumbull, Connecticut, sixty-one-year-old Arnold Russo bought a .25 caliber semiautomatic pistol to use as protection against robbers in his Bridgeport variety store. He wanted to show his wife how to use the gun. He handed it to her and told her that in order to get the feel of the gun she should squeeze the trigger. Mrs. Russo did as he said and the gun went off, killing him.

Each year some 1,500 Americans are killed in accidents involving guns. Between 11,000 and 12,000 more use handguns to commit suicide, while 6,000 people use other firearms to kill themselves. Among these suicides are 3,000 children. The number of suicides among teenagers is rising at an alarming rate.

Why? There are no simple answers. President Reagan's former press secretary James Brady is today a leading champion of gun control. He worries about the effect of T.V. violence, which exploits bloodshed without conveying its agony. "Children are exposed to gun violence at such an early age that they simply cannot distinguish between reality and make-believe," says Brady. When they enter adolescence, which is a time of self-questioning and self-doubt, thoughts of suicide may arise.

Suicide. An estimated 3.6 million high school students consider taking their lives every year, according to a 1990 study by the Centers for Disease Control. But there is a wide gulf between thinking about it and doing it. Less than one tenth of one percent who think about it act on the impulse.

One important difference between that small fraction and those who do not kill themselves is the presence of a gun in the home. This view comes from the Western Psychiatric Institute and Clinic of Pittsburgh and the University of Pittsburgh Graduate School of Public Health. Their researches concluded that "a suicidal teenager living in a home with an easily accessible gun is more likely to commit suicide than a suicidal teenager living in a home where no gun is present."

They also found that "suicidal teenagers who have been drinking alcohol are five times more likely to use guns than any other suicide method." It should be noted that the leading health problem among U.S. adolescents today is alcoholism.

In Vermont a suicidal seventeen-year-old boy got

drunk and walked down the center divider of a main boulevard, lurching into the lanes of oncoming traffic. Cars screeched to a halt to avoid him. A man shepherded him to the safety of the sidewalk. "Hey kid," he told the young man, "if you really want to kill yourself, a gun is quicker and easier." And he sold him a secondhand pistol for fifty dollars.

The pistol lay in the youth's drawer for over a year. Although friends and family members were aware of it, they were reluctant to take it away. Then, around Christmas time, a girl he liked turned him down for a date to a party. His parents were out and he sat up in his room drinking alone. When his mother came home she found him dead, with a bullet from the rusty pistol in his brain.

Guns in Society. Firearms-control advocates point out that guns do not exist in a vacuum. Rather, they are the wild card in a society rife with problems of drugs and alcohol, domestic disputes, and emotional instability. Their presence, they say, always has the potential to turn an unpleasant situation into a tragic one.

Most murders in America are committed by people who know their victim. During arguments, pressures build, anger erupts. A gun can make that anger lethal. The fury felt by a parent toward a son or daughter can turn murderous if a gun is handy. A quarrel over a card game can escalate into homicide. Landlord-tenant disputes, lovers' quarrels, arguments between neighbors—so many tensions can turn deadly when a gun is present. Over and over again gun-control advocates see new evidence of this.

It makes them question the gun "tradition" in rural areas of the country. They ask, how many people today really use guns to kill for food on anything approaching a regular basis? They wonder if hunting for food is really a necessity. The suffering of animals that are wounded but not killed is mentioned. The killing of endangered species (with guns that are legal) is deplored. So too is the number of innocent people who are shot and wounded or killed during the various hunting seasons every year.

They also point out that the highest alcoholism rates in the country occur in sparsely populated states like Vermont, Arizona, and Wyoming. In the West, in particular, this has combined with a masculine firearms culture to create an escalating carnage that, as a percentage of population, is as alarming as that of the big cities. Some Westerners wear gunbelts as casually as they wear ten-gallon hats, and carry shotguns as nonchalantly as tote bags.

In one small Arizona town on a Sunday morning, a man accosted a young woman he'd been dating as she was about to enter a church. An argument ensued over her having gone out with someone else the night before. His voice got louder and he raised the shotgun he was carrying and brandished it. The woman told him angrily to stop acting like Rambo. Suddenly the gun went off. The young woman was rushed to the hospital with her leg in shreds, while the man was still trying to explain to the arresting officers that he hadn't ever really meant to shoot.

Jealousy is rarely accompanied by good judgment. It often involves anger. When someone is rejected, he or she may want to get even, to reject the other person in return. Murder is the ultimate rejection. In the instant it takes to *feel* that, a gun makes the act possible.

The Coalition to Stop Gun Violence and other such groups want to lessen that possibility. An average of 35,000 people die as a result of gunshot wounds in the United States every year. Do guns kill people? The answer for them is another question: If guns had not been available, how many of those 35,000 victims would still be alive today?

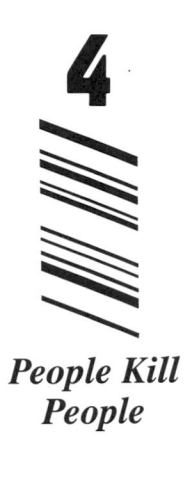

People Kill
People

Guns can help prevent crimes. That is a key position of those opposed to gun control. They point out that mounting violence and budget cuts have stretched police power thin. Legitimately armed citizens, they say, must take the streets back from the criminals, must protect themselves and their neighborhoods. Statistical evidence and persuasive examples are selected to back up this conviction.

Gun advocates point to drops in the crime rates of both urban and suburban neighborhoods where legally armed street patrols have made themselves a highly visible presence. Drug dealers and other criminals avoid areas where they are met with firepower equal to their own. They argue that police records show that individuals, whether organized in groups or on their own, can deter crime with firearms—particularly handguns.

Guns for Defense. The criminals themselves agree. As part of a three-year study by the U.S. Department of Justice, criminals in prisons across the nation were interviewed. Sixty percent feared being shot by an armed citizen more than being shot by the police. Fifty-three percent did not commit a specific crime because they were afraid the victim was armed. Fifty-seven percent were scared off by an armed victim who either brandished a gun or actually fired it.

One such case involved eleven-year-old Jason Green of Houston, Texas. Home alone one night, he heard noises in the house. Arming himself with his father's shotgun, he investigated and caught a burglar in the act. Just then his mother pulled up outside in the family car. Fearing the burglar might harm his mother, Jason fired. His mother reacted by bursting into the house and firing her revolver. Hit by bullets from both guns, the burglar was killed.

Jason's mother, like Jason, was defending her home against an intruder. There are about 645,000 defensive uses of handguns each year, according to Gary Kleck, a professor at Florida State University. He bases his figure on several surveys on handgun use, including one done for an organization that favors banning handguns. Kleck also concluded that handguns used "in self-defense, or some other legally justified cause" kill between 1,500 and 2,800 criminals every year. If other types of firearms besides handguns are included, then over 1 million law-abiding citizens use guns for self-protection annually.

U.S. Justice Department data indicate such firearms use is effective. Armed citizens are twice as likely to avoid injury during a robbery as unarmed victims. Only one in seven of those armed are hurt as opposed to one in three who are unarmed. (This contradicts the police experience cited in the previous chapter.)

The right of these victims to defend themselves with guns is most staunchly championed by the National Rifle Association, the leading (but not the only) organization opposed to putting restrictions on gun sales. The NRA

A young visitor to a National Rifle Association convention checks out a .44 Magnum pistol equipped with a hunting scope.

boasts 2.9 million members and is growing. Much of its support comes from the 60 to 65 million Americans who own firearms. Many of them keep guns for reasons of self-defense. These people consider a gun to be an "equalizer."

That's what it was in Ft. Wayne, Indiana, when an eighty-nine-year-old woman was manhandled by a hooded burglar who broke into her house. In the bedroom, her ninety-one-year-old husband heard her struggling, grabbed his shotgun, and hurried to the rescue. When the burglar saw the gun, he fled. The woman summed it up for the local *News Sentinel* reporter: "The gun saved us."

The incident illustrates the major point of the NRA: a gun is the only really effective protection the weakest members of our society have against those who would prey on them. Elderly people in particular are increasingly being targeted by young toughs as easy victims. They don't have the strength to fight back, and often their bodies aren't able to recover from the beatings they endure while being robbed. For the elderly and the disabled, a small handgun is often the only defense.

It is also a defense for women vulnerable to rape. Some years back, in Orlando, Florida, the number of rapes rose over a twelve-month period from 12.8 per 100,000 to 35.9 per 100,000. Women in Orlando were afraid to go out alone, even in the daytime. Demands mounted that something be done to deal with both the threat itself and the fear it was causing.

Something was done. The Orlando Police Department set up a program to train women to use handguns. Over three thousand women armed themselves and took training. As a result, Orlando rape figures dropped to 4.1 per 100,000—a 90 percent decline from the previous high. Similar programs in Detroit and Highland Park, Michigan, and Montgomery, Alabama, saw impressive reductions in crimes against women, including both rape and robbery.

Today's woman has taken note of this. Whether she is a housewife or a working woman, young or middle-aged, living in an urban, suburban, or rural area, her consciousness has been raised to the threat of rape and the role of firearms in dealing with it. A Gallup poll revealed that the number of female gun-owners rose by 53 percent in the mid-1980s. Since then women have been joining gun clubs in increasing numbers, taking instruction in gun use, perfecting their skills at target shooting, and buying handguns. Indeed, in many parts of America today women buy as many new, legally sold handguns as men do. And many women's groups hand out pamphlets and offer advice on the use of guns to prevent victimization by rape and other crimes.

One woman victim decided on her own that she had had enough. A fifty-one-year-old resident of Los Angeles, California, twice raped by the same man, she purchased a handgun and took lessons to learn how to use it. When the man returned a third time, she shot him dead.

Gun Safety. The lessons she took were important, according to those who speak out for the right to bear arms. Gun ownership involves the obligation to learn about firearms. All gun owners, men as well as women, must know how to use the gun, how to secure it, how to store it. Safety is best served not by depriving people of weapons, they say, but rather by teaching gun owners how to handle them.

Groups like the NRA back up this position with programs and publications designed to show guns as user-friendly and to make even young children familiar with them. The "Eddie Eagle" coloring book program for kindergarten through sixth grade has reached some 1.6

*Members of a women's gun club in
Springfield, Massachusetts, pose at
a target range. Growing numbers
of women have taken up shooting
for sport as well as defense.*

million youngsters in the past two years. Some law enforcement agencies have worked with the program to broadcast public service TV messages teaching gun safety to children. Those who believe that familiarity prevents accidents claim this is a factor in a 50 percent drop in fatal mishaps involving guns and minors between 1974 and 1989. (Their opponents deny this.)

Such familiarity is at the core of basic NRA Gun Safety Rules, as follows:

- Store guns so they are not accessible to unauthorized persons.
- Always keep the gun unloaded until ready to use.
- Be sure the gun is safe to operate.
- Know how to safely use the gun.
- Use only the correct ammunition for your gun.
- Always keep the gun pointed in a safe direction.
- Never hand someone a gun unless the chamber is open and empty.
- Always keep your finger off the trigger until ready to shoot.

Fighting Crime. Gun advocates deplore the rising violence among American adolescents. But they point out that in most cases guns are not involved. Murder, in particular, takes many forms and may involve a variety of weapons.

On February 16, 1992, in Clifton, New Jersey, four suburban boys ages fourteen to eighteen killed a schoolmate while reciting a prayer with him. The perpetrators did not use a firearm, but rather a length of cord to commit the homicide. A 1992 study on injuries and deaths in the United States by the Center for Disease Control shows that while 20 percent of U.S. high school students surveyed said they carried a weapon at least once during the preceding month for protection, or because they might need it in a fight, in only one out of five cases was that weapon a firearm.

Only a small percentage of today's youth are disturbed and violent. Opponents of firearms controls do not see them as relying on guns to commit assault and murder. They insist that the availability of firearms is not the significant factor in the pattern of violence.

Besides, those guns that are used by both youthful and adult criminals are usually bought illegally. Placing restrictions on purchases of guns by honest citizens from reputable dealers will not lessen the ability of criminals to purchase them on the black market. It will only keep prospective victims from protecting themselves. This is the answer of firearms advocates to those who would legislate gun control to fight crime. But it is not their only argument against such legislation.

Anti-gun laws, they say, would be a spur to the already existing black market in firearms. As Prohibition did with liquor, bans on guns—whether all guns or just handguns or just semiautomatic weapons—would create a lucrative market for enterprising smugglers. Not only criminals but also law-abiding citizens wishing to protect themselves would end up as customers of such operations. Accidents would happen more frequently as cheap, jerrybuilt weapons replaced those once made by reputable gun manufacturers. Police resources would be strained by the additional burden of having to deal with turf wars among illegal gun sellers similar to those already going on among dope peddlers.

The NRA alternative to gun control is a program called CrimeStrike that demands an end to revolving-door justice. It calls for spotlighting violent repeat offenders and giving them long jail sentences. It would expose the conviction and sentencing records of lenient prosecutors and judges with the aim of having these officials removed. CrimeStrike would end plea bargaining, which downgrades charges against armed criminals. It would repeal laws that its supporters believe favor felons, and organize voters against politicians who oppose stiff sentences and building needed prisons. It would increase funding for police departments and other law enforcement agencies.

Guns for Sport. The NRA also warns that the gun-control legislation proposed so far will be only the beginning of restrictions that will interfere with legitimate sports and hobbies. It cites surveys indicating that some 33 million Americans use guns for hunting. Over 7 million use them for target shooting. And over 2.5 million collect guns the way other people collect baseball cards or antique pewter.

No doubt, there is a large segment of the American population for whom firearms are primarily agents of fun. In densely populated areas, both cities and suburbs, the fun is usually restricted to indoor shooting ranges, weekend flea markets where guns are featured as collectibles, and periodic vacation hunting trips. But in small towns and rural areas where there are wide open spaces, gun sports are more often regular outdoor activities.

In such places, hunting is a time-honored practice, whether done out of necessity for food or as a sport. The game is eaten in either case. Hunters insist their prey suffers far less than domestic animals stampeded through the chutes of slaughterhouses to be neatly quartered, wrapped, and sold at meat counters. Gun hunting thins out herds that would otherwise suffer cruel deaths from freezing and starvation. There are 25 million hunting licenses sold every year in the United States, and most of them are purchased in those sparsely populated areas where 72 percent of the households have guns.

Many hunters oppose restrictions on firearms, seeing guns as an essential part of their sport.

Many people in rural America view guns as key to their life-style. In the South and Southwest, where such attitudes are most popular, people point out that human beings are natural hunters and always have been. Animals kill animals for food; that is nature's way. Life-forms compete for survival. Tools devised by the human brain ensure the survival of our species in this competition. Some of these tools are firearms.

The "fun" of guns is not confined to hunting. Outdoor target shooting—skeet and trap with clay pigeons fired at by those who don't like to shoot at living creatures—is a popular activity in some states, such as Arizona. Outdoor as well as indoor ranges offer Western-style shootout contests involving gunshooter silhouettes and semiautomatic pistols.

These silhouettes have circles inside circles for scoring rings. A contestant standing fifty yards away has two minutes and forty-five seconds to fire twenty-four rounds from four pre-set positions. Ten to fifteen bullets are fired with each squeeze of the trigger. Not everybody can compete at this level, but it is one goal among many for those to whom shooting is a hobby.

Most pleasure shooting, however, doesn't involve high-tech firearms. It's done with more conventional pistols. Nor does it involve contests or target ranges. It's more a matter of getting outdoors and away from people and popping away at cans or bottles. This is called plinking. According to Robert E. Jensen, president of Jensen's Guns and Ammo in Tucson, Arizona, plinking accounts for 60 percent of all the ammunition he sells. One of his customers, James Jennings, says that on most weekends he fires two hundred bullets plinking in the desert, because "I enjoy it, just going out and shooting a nice quality weapon."

Most of those who go plinking believe that in our increasingly violent world, a firearm by itself has no morality. The person who uses it determines whether it will be a force for good or evil. Good people must have the same access to that firearm as society's misfits do. And they view plinking itself as evidence that what they have always said is true: Guns don't kill people; people kill people.

Guns, Guns, and More Guns

A burglar broke into the home of Thomas Williamson of Collinsville, Illinois, in June 1988. Hearing him moving around, Williamson got his gun and investigated. The burglar was trying to hide on the stairs when Williamson came face-to-face with him. Williamson shot and killed the intruder. A police investigation revealed that the dead man had just been released from prison. No charges were pressed against Williamson, who authorities said was "protecting himself and his dwelling." The weapon he had used to do that was a .357 Magnum revolver.

Shortly after the record stock-market plunge of October 19, 1987, Arthur Kane walked into the Tamiami Gun Shop in Miami, Florida, and made a purchase. Kane was a disbarred lawyer. He had testified against his accomplices in a case involving insurance fraud, served a short jail term, and was then given a new identity and relocated under a federal government witness-protection program. Kane had no problem buying a gun because a recent Florida state law had wiped out all local gun-control ordinances and made it legal for any adult to buy one. Kane took the gun to the Merrill Lynch brokerage house that had sold him his sagging stocks. There Kane killed the branch manager, wounded his personal stockbroker, and then killed himself. His weapon, too, was a .357 Magnum.

The .357 Magnum revolver is a high-powered fire-arm. *High-powered* means that the bullet it fires travels at a speed roughly twice as fast as the average revolver bullet. It has an impact greater than that of a Winchester .44 rifle. A bullet from a .357 Magnum will usually go right on through its target to do maximum damage to whatever happens to be behind it.

The cylinder of the .357 holds six cartridges. The revolver has a real kick when fired. For this reason law enforcement officials who use it usually brace the hand holding the gun with the other hand to steady it. The .357 Magnum was made famous by Clint Eastwood in the *Dirty Harry* movies. Over the past fifteen years it has remained one of the more popular handguns.

Handguns. There are three kinds of handguns. Single-action *revolvers* fire only one shot at a time. To fire again the shooter must pull back the hammer to rotate the cylinder holding the bullets before squeezing the trigger. (Double-action revolvers also fire one shot, but there is no need to cock the hammer.)

The second category is the *semiautomatic*. It has no cylinder as a revolver does, but rather a magazine to hold the bullets. The magazine is stored in the barrel of the weapon. With a tightly coiled spring pushing the bullets into the firing chamber, reloading is lightning fast. A semiautomatic usually doesn't have a hammer. If it does, it is reset mechanically (rather than by hand) as the trigger is pulled.

Some semiautomatics have clips that can hold up to thirty bullets. They can be fired as rapidly as the trigger

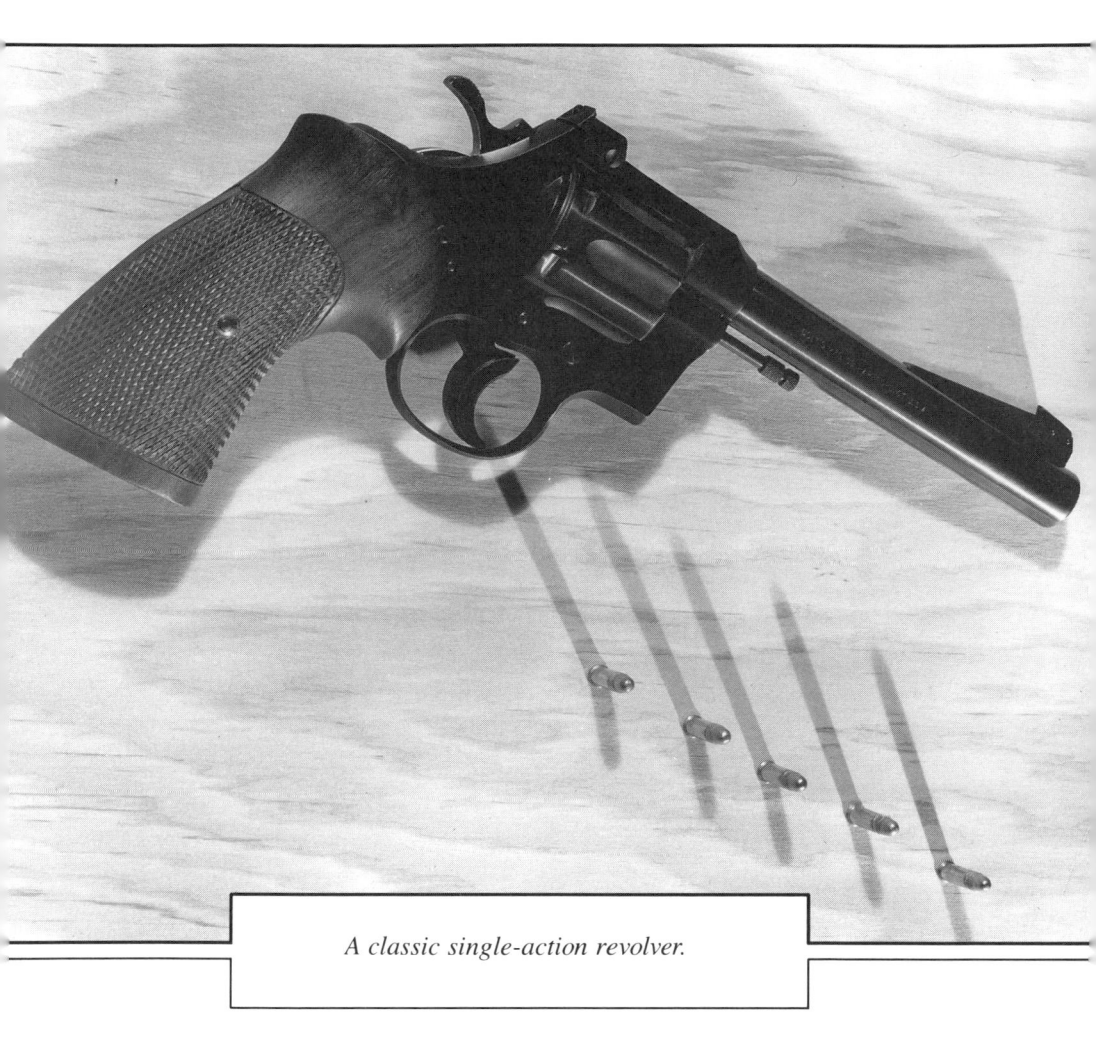

A classic single-action revolver.

finger can move. Such rapid fire can spray a wide area, although sometimes at the expense of accuracy and force of impact.

This spray effect has been the subject of controversy among law enforcement and other government officials in cities across the country. Typical is the dispute during the spring and summer of 1992 between the New York City Patrolmen's Benevolent Association, backed by the New York State Senate and Governor Mario Cuomo, on one side and New York City's Mayor David Dinkins and Police Commissioner Lee Brown on the other. The conflict centered on the Glock 19, a late-model lightweight semi-automatic pistol that holds fifteen rounds of hard-nosed 9mm ammo. Rank-and-file policemen, facing similar weapons in the hands of criminals, had Smith & Wesson .38s holding just six bullets capable of being fired only one at a time. They insisted they needed the Glock 19 to defend themselves. The mayor and police commissioner, citing the high population density of New York City, saw the Glock 19 as a threat to innocent bystanders because its rapid-fire high-powered bullets would pass through targets and spray wide areas. As of this writing, a compromise "test program" that would allow limited use of the Glock 19 has been hammered out between the P.B.A. and the commissioner (who shortly thereafter announced his resignation), but has not yet been approved by the state legislature.

Fully *automatic pistols*, the third type of handgun, are usually jerry-built. The mechanism of a semiautomatic is altered so that, if the trigger is pulled just once and held back, the gun will rapid-fire one bullet after another like a machine gun. The result is even less accurate than that of a semiautomatic, but more devastating in terms of the area it covers and the innocent bystanders put at risk.

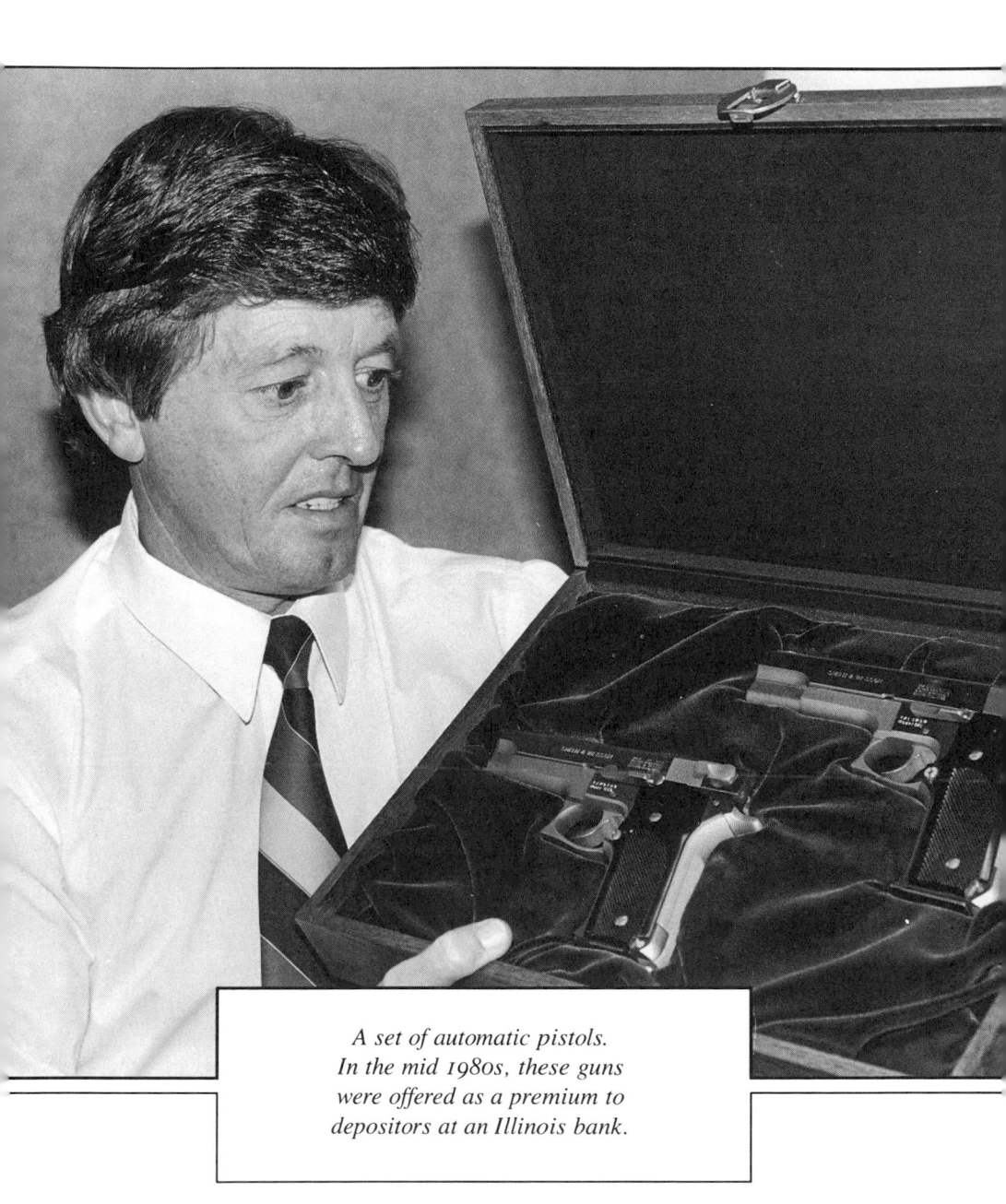

*A set of automatic pistols.
In the mid 1980s, these guns
were offered as a premium to
depositors at an Illinois bank.*

These three groups of handguns are what some people want to regulate and others would like to ban altogether. The National Rifle Association, which opposes such legislation (except bans on jerry-built automatics), estimates that there are approximately 60 to 65 million of these handguns in the United States. Each year for the past several years that figure has increased by 2 million or more. Because the total keeps growing, both the legitimate selling price and the black-market price of handguns has been dropping.

"These guns are not wearing out," according to William B. Ruger, Sr., chairman of Sturm, Ruger & Company, a leading manufacturer of handguns. He adds that "used guns are competing with our new production. People are buying guns for half the money."

Cheap handguns have long been known as Saturday Night Specials because more crimes in cities take place between six P.M. Saturday and four A.M. Sunday than at any other time. Muggings, stickups of cab drivers, robberies of homes and apartments while dwellers are out for the evening, violence stemming from passion and jealousy—all these and other crimes involving handguns are much more frequent on Saturday nights. It is then that people drink alcohol, inhibitions are lowered, guards are down, and predators are on the lookout for crimes of opportunity. These lawbreakers are most often armed with Saturday Night Specials. Depending on the city and the particular model, they pay between $50 and $350 for one.

The Specials can be revolvers, semiautomatics, or semiautomatics converted into fully automatic pistols. Because they are cheaply made, they don't have the firepower of high-tech guns like the .357 Magnum. Many use soft lead bullets instead of ones with metal casings like those fired by high-power pistols. A metal bullet hits harder, travels farther, and penetrates cleanly, leaving behind a small, neat hole with little damage to the area surrounding it. But a soft lead bullet moves slowly, and when it strikes it mushrooms, shedding fragments and tearing ragged holes. If the former were to strike a person in the shoulder, it might wound that person seriously. The latter, because of its tendency to shatter on impact, send bone chips flying, and sever arteries, is more likely to kill the person.

Over half the murders in the United States every year are committed with handguns, the great majority of them Saturday Night Specials. Handgun Control Inc., the leading group lobbying for federal legislation to restrict the spread of handguns, wants laws passed that would prohibit the manufacture, importation, and sale of Saturday Night Specials. Backing their position up with data on the use of Saturday Night Specials in drug-related street crimes, violence against police, domestic shootings, and murders, Handgun Control singles out Specials not only because they are cheap to buy, but also because they are easy to conceal. That means a minimum of warning to potential victims. Handgun Control would like the carrying of a concealed pistol to be made a federal crime.

The group has also focused on so-called *undetectable* handguns with plastic parts, like the Glock 17, allegedly favored by terrorists. Such pistols have been disassembled, passed through airport scanners, and then reassembled and used in airliner hijackings. They might also be slipped through metal detectors in inner-city schools, where the threat of a shooting is ever-present. Handgun Control worked to push a bill through Congress banning the sale of undetectable handguns. But the bill that finally passed compromised by exempting plastic Specials with metal parts. Since most plastic Specials do have some metal parts, the law is ineffective.

A particular target of Handgun Control is the bulk sale of Specials at discount, or wholesale, prices. They cite police and FBI evidence that this has increased the profitable gun-running trade across state lines. Dealing in large quantities makes for large profits and floods neighborhoods most vulnerable to violence with the most guns. Handgun Control calls for a strictly enforced federal ban on bulk sales of the cheap Specials.

The NRA and its anti-gun control allies do not agree with any of this. They point out that "Saturday Night Special" is simply another name for an inexpensive pistol. Making these guns illegal would discriminate against the poor. It would put guns out of their reach, while people who are better off financially could still ensure their self-defense with more costly weapons. This is particularly unfair since poor people are the very ones most likely to live in high-crime areas, they say.

The NRA considers the idea of a law against concealing weapons to be silly. A handgun is small. How can you transport it without concealing it? Should it be held in the lap, unwrapped, on the commuter train? Is the suburban housewife concealing her gun if it's in the glove compartment of her car? Should it be on the dashboard within reach of curious children?

It was the anti-gun control lobby that got Congress to water down the bill banning plastic handguns. They agreed to a ban on undetectable firearms after experts testified before Congress that there were no 100 percent plastic handguns on the market. Their position was that to ban all guns with plastic parts would be to once again discriminate against the cheaper models.

As to a law against bulk sales of Saturday Night Specials, firearms manufacturers protest that this would be an undemocratic restraint of free trade. They point out that many more people are killed by cars every year than are killed by guns. Yet no one suggests that car manufacturers be prevented from offering dealers multi-sale discounts. Government doesn't interfere with car makers' sales, or hold them responsible when a drunk driver kills a pedestrian. Why should it interfere with marketing by gun manufacturers or blame them when some criminal, who probably bought his or her weapon illegally, hurts someone with it?

The argument over Saturday Night Specials is a matter of focus. The gun-control advocates look at increasing violence and mounting numbers of victims and say the spread of these guns must be stopped. The anti-control advocates look at the 30 to 35 million legitimate handgun owners in the United States and ask, What about their right to protect themselves?

Another argument has centered on the Intratec Tec-9 semiautomatic pistol, which retails for $260. Police call the Tec-9, with its ventilated five-inch barrel, thirty-two-round magazine, and two-hand grip, an "assault pistol." This type of heavy-duty semiautomatic was recently outlawed in New York City.

The Tec-9 is the weapon of preference for drug dealers in New York, according to Lieutenant Kenneth McCann, a cocommander of the New York City Police Department Joint Firearms Task Force. He went on to compare it to a fully automatic Uzi, or machine gun.

In 1990–91, the Federal Bureau of Alcohol, Tobacco and Firearms traced 1,546 Tec-9s used in crimes, making it the leading criminally used assault weapon in the United States. Many Tec-9s have special features like silencers, shrouds to keep the gun barrel cooled down during sustained rapid fire, a special lubrication to increase bullet speed, telescopic sights (until recent years only used

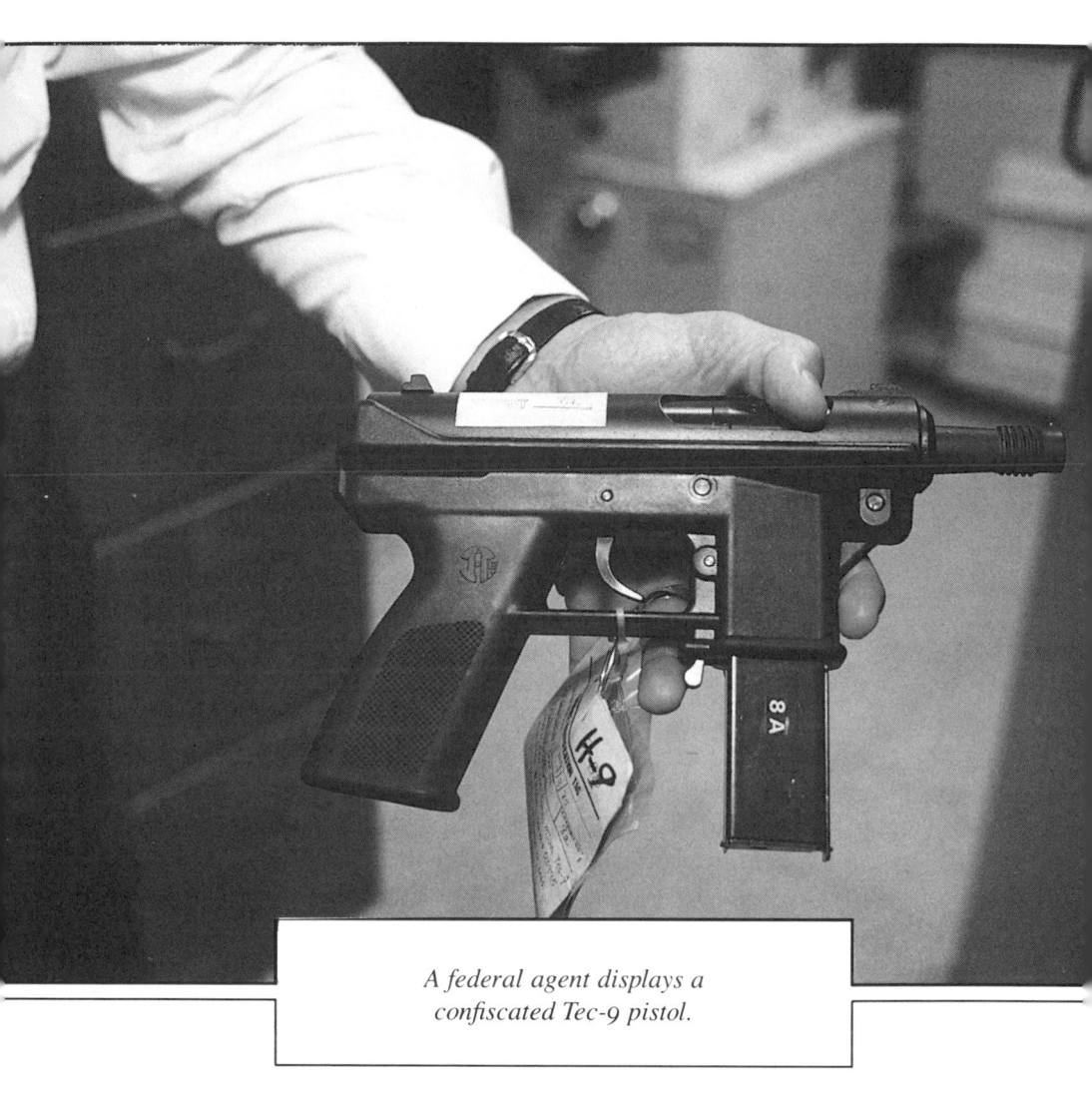

*A federal agent displays a
confiscated Tec-9 pistol.*

on long guns), and grips that have "excellent resistance to fingerprints," according to the Intratec brochure. Other assault pistols offer similar options.

Superintendent of Chicago Police LeRoy Martin wants weapons like the Tec-9 to be banned in Illinois because "they are designed to spray whole groups of people, and they can be equipped with extra clips for extra firepower, or can be modified in a short time to be fully automatic." He views them as a threat to police and insists they "serve no useful purpose."

But Jerry Ahearn, who writes for weapons magazines, disagrees. "This gun is primarily used by good, honest citizens," insists Ahearn. "If needed in home defense, it looks scary enough that the intruder would probably take off and run." This is also the point of view of an Intratec advertisement featuring a father teaching his small son to shoot an assault pistol.

Intratec's marketing and sales director, Mike Solo, calls the Tec-9 an excellent plinking gun because it holds thirty-two rounds, so "you can fill it up and plink a little bit more." He also claims that the Tec-9 is used by some U.S. police antiterrorism squads and by military forces in Third World countries, who say its intimidating appearance helps with crowd control. While admitting that Tec-9s may end up being used illegally, Solo insists that the primary customer is "John Q. Public, the average Joe."

Long Guns. In rural areas, however, John Q. Public is more likely to buy a shotgun or a rifle than a beefed-up handgun. Because most of these guns aren't registered, accurate statistics aren't available, according to the Federal Bureau of Alcohol, Tobacco and Firearms. But they greatly outnumber handguns. Of special concern are semiautomatic or fully automatic assault rifles. These guns make up only a small percentage of the total, but their number is growing rapidly due to the illegal smuggling of assault rifles into the country.

These guns are a far cry from the traditional shotgun used to hunt possum and rabbit and other small game in the South and Southwest. Because these animals move fast and are hard to hit, a shotgun is favored over a rifle because it fires a number of small projectiles called shot rather than a single bullet. This shot sprays out over a much wider area, making it easier to hit the prey.

Shotguns can be fired only once (twice if they are double-barreled) before reloading, which is accomplished by a bolt, hinge, or pump mechanism. Double-barreled triggers can be pulled quickly, one after the other, which further widens the target area. There are also semiautomatic shotguns which reload mechanically when the shot is fired. Gas from the burning gunpowder provides the compression to do this.

Sometimes the barrels of shotguns are sawed off. This is done for two reasons. The sawed-off barrel will deliver the widest possible spray of shot at short range. This can cause more damage over a wider area with a single shot than any other weapon. Also, the sawed-off shotgun is easy to conceal under a jacket or dress or even inside trousers. Sawed-off shotguns have long been the weapon of choice for criminals in rural areas.

Rifles are more accurate and have greater range than shotguns. As with a shotgun, there can only be one cartridge in the firing chamber at a time. The reloading process is also similar.

Primarily, rifles are used for hunting larger game such as deer. The most powerful rifles are used in big-game hunting. Every kind of rifle is used in target shooting, an increasingly popular sport with Americans.

A U.S. Customs Department official
with a confiscated semiautomatic
shotgun, or "street sweeper."

High-powered rifles propel bullets over long distances. Telescopic sights make them extremely accurate. This is an obvious asset in hunting, but it is also what makes them attractive to assassins. Both President John F. Kennedy and civil rights leader Martin Luther King, Jr., were murdered with rifles.

Most lethal are the semiautomatic and fully automatic rifles. One of the most popular of these a few years back was the Soviet-made AK-47 assault rifle. While the semiautomatic version released only one bullet with each trigger-pull, the reload action was designed to make repeat shots particularly easy.

In 1989 a mentally disturbed drifter named Patrick Purdy took his AK-47 to a Stockton, California, elementary school playground. He opened fire on the children there, killing five between the ages of six and nine, and wounding another twenty-nine. Then he killed himself.

Purdy had not modified his legally purchased AK-47 to make it fully automatic. If he had, he could have loosed up to 900 rounds of ammunition a minute, many times the 106 bullets he actually did fire. Those who oppose gun control on the grounds that it doesn't work point out that modifying the weapon would have been against the law. But how likely was it, they ask, that this would have deterred the madman?

Nevertheless, reaction to the tragedy favored the gun-control lobbyists. After the Stockton massacre Congress made it illegal to import the AK-47. American gun manufacturers rushed to fill the void. They copied the AK-47 design, and sales of the knock-offs have soared. These guns are particularly popular with shootists at outdoor ranges, among paramilitary groups, and for training at survivalist camps. These enthusiasts applauded when the NRA successfully opposed recent efforts to outlaw the manufacture and sale of assault rifles by U.S. companies.

These AK-47 rifles, made in China, were impounded by U.S. Customs officials after imports of such weapons were banned in 1989.

The NRA pointed out that according to an FBI Uniform Crime Report less than 1 percent of crimes involve long guns and that less than one tenth of that 1 percent involve semiautomatic rifles or shotguns.

But the gun-control advocates are still demanding such a ban. Will they get it? Should they? The debate continues, and the number of assault weapons in the United States grows.

How Much Control?

Gun control means different things to different people. There is a wide range of positions, with extremes at either end. Some would ban the manufacture, import, distribution, sale, and possession of any and all firearms. They would even take away guns from police forces and have officers armed only with batons, or billy clubs.

Their reasoning is that this would lower the level of violence. Police without firearms would be less threatening to emotionally upset lawbreakers. Many professional criminals would be persuaded that they needn't carry guns for self-defense. Young people, who commit the majority of crimes, would have more respect for police officers. The models for this point of view are the police officers of Great Britain and the Republic of Ireland. They do not carry firearms and often do not bother carrying batons, and yet are held in the highest esteem.

The commander of the Central Police Station in Dundee, Scotland, was asked how unarmed police cope with Scotland's mounting drug problem. (Nearby Edinburgh is considered the drug capital of Europe, and disputes among dealers are a growing concern.) He responded that Scottish police had learned from the U.S. experience that guns are not the answer. "We may not do any better than U.S. authorities," he observed, "but we don't think we will do any worse."

The officer spoke from personal experience. While participating in an exchange program with the Washington, D.C., police department, he was paired with a Washington policeman in a patrol car. "One night," he recalled, "we got an emergency call to respond to a gunfire incident. Five other patrol cars also responded. Ten or more police officers with drawn guns were independently searching a maze of dark alleys for an armed perpetrator, none really knowing where the others might be. The danger was obvious to me. I went back to the patrol car and stayed there."

British and Irish police officers do not understand the routine carrying of guns by American lawmen. Their rule is that only special squads may be issued firearms, and then only in special situations. Three levels of command must approve the issuing of the weapons. In an extreme emergency the highest ranking officer on duty may release guns to special squads, but he does this knowing that he will routinely have to justify to a board of inquiry both the order and any injuries resulting from the use of the firearms.

A Dublin policeman, speaking in the aftermath of the April 1992 Los Angeles riots, summed it up best. "Officers must set an example," he said. "Guns solve nothing."

At the other extreme are those who insist there should be no restrictions at all where firearms are concerned. They do not think that any weapon, from a small "lady's" revolver to a hand-held missile launcher or bazooka, should be regulated in any way. This view extends to types of ammunition like steel cartridges, which can pierce the bulletproof vests worn by police.

They oppose any kind of licensing of guns or restriction of sales. Anybody, including convicted felons, should have the constitutional right to buy, sell, or trade any kind of gun. The rationale for this position has been voiced by Aaron Zelman of Milwaukee, who founded a group of about two thousand members for the Preservation of Firearms Ownership. Says Zelman: "We view the primary reason for ownership of weapons as helping to defend the nation against those who would destroy freedom, and of course personal defense."

The majority of people on both sides of the question do not subscribe to either a total ban of firearms or complete freedom from regulation. Rather, depending on which position they lean toward and why, they take stands on an issue-by-issue basis. Some of these issues are themselves very complex, and there are many fine points to be considered. Debates arising from them have been heated, and most recent legislation on the federal level has passed only after such debates have dragged on for long periods of time.

Federal Laws. The first federal gun statute, still in effect, was passed in 1927. It forbade shipping concealable firearms (handguns) through the U.S. mails and was followed in 1934 by the National Firearms Act, which restricted sales and ownership of machine guns and similar warlike weapons.

In 1968, following a rash of assassinations and assassination attempts, the Federal Gun Control Act became law. It outlawed mail-order sales of *all* guns, narrowly limited interstate transport, and banned sales by dealers to out-of-state residents, convicted criminals, and drug users. The seller was required to confirm the name and address of the buyer and to keep careful records of what guns and ammunition were bought and by whom. (The Federal Bureau of Alcohol, Tobacco and Firearms would monitor these records.) According to the U.S. Supreme Court, the purpose of the law was to reduce crime by keeping "firearms out of the hands of those not legally entitled to possess them because of age, criminal background, or incompetency."

On May 19, 1986, eighteen years after the passage of the Federal Gun Control Act, it was altered by adoption of the Firearms Owners Protection Act, which was itself amended later that year (the McClure-Volkmer Amendments). Together these revisions made it legal to transport guns through states that might have interfered with such shipments by voiding all state and local laws forbidding the transport of unloaded firearms. They made sales of long guns to out-of-state residents legal unless local law forbade them.

McClure-Volkmer created loopholes for those, including some with criminal records, who might be barred from buying a gun. It limited the government's ability to seize guns that had been or might be used in crimes. The oversight ability of the Bureau of Alcohol, Tobacco and Firearms was restricted. The Amendments eliminated the license requirement for ammunition dealers. They reduced the record-keeping requirements for firearms dealers.

These changes weakened the original 1968 Gun Control Act. At the same time they dealt with some very difficult clashes between rights. So does the pro-gun control Brady Bill, which as previously noted became tied up in Congress.

The Brady Bill singles out handguns for regulation. Handgun Control Inc. has been the leader in the campaign for its passage. The organization is headed by Sarah Brady, the wife of James Brady. The gun used in the assassination attempt that left James Brady disabled was a .22 caliber RG revolver that cost $47. The would-be assassin, John W. Hinckley, Jr., had bought it at Rocky's Pawn Shop in Dallas, Texas. He had filled out a federal form to buy two such guns and was able to leave the shop with both after paying for them.

Waiting Periods and Instant Checks. The Brady Bill would require a specific waiting period for anyone applying to buy a handgun before he or she may take possession of it. During that period a background check would be run on the buyer. "Had a waiting period been in effect," insists Sarah Brady, "John Hinckley would not have had the opportunity to buy the gun he used."

Opponents of the Brady Bill challenge that. They point out that Hinckley bought his weapons in October 1980, almost six months before the assassination attempt. Just before that he was arrested for trying to smuggle a different gun aboard a plane in Nashville, Tennessee. A police background check was run on him at that time, but it turned up nothing. He paid a small fine and was released. Neither a waiting period nor a background check would have prevented Hinckley from buying the gun he used to shoot James Brady, say gun advocates.

According to the NRA, "Waiting periods invite arbitrary denials based on faulty or incomplete records, discourage law-abiding citizens from obtaining firearms, and have proved a costly waste of law enforcement resources that could have otherwise been utilized to fight crime and apprehend criminals." The organization adds that "a waiting period scheme redirects police from crime fighting to . . . snooping into the private lives of law-abiding citizens buying guns through licensed firearms dealers." This makes it "safer for criminals."

*Gun-control advocate Sarah Brady and
her husband, Jim Brady, who was
disabled by a gunman attempting to
assassinate former President Reagan,
meet with Senate leaders in 1989.*

However, the NRA does favor an "instant telephone check" system which would rely on a centralized federal data bank receiving input from all law enforcement agencies across the country. This would separate criminals from legitimate citizens on the spot without interfering with the transaction. It would interfere with neither the seller's business nor the buyer's need for a firearm.

Opposition to this compromise, however, comes from many sources. In a time of budget cuts, many Congressional legislators feel the cost of establishing such a centralized data bank would be exorbitant. Those most strongly against gun control claim such checks would interfere with purchases by 12 percent to 16 percent of legitimate gun buyers. The data bank would automatically place this group in a gray area and they would have to go through a second checking process involving fingerprinting, which could take several weeks.

On the other side, many see the instant check as doing away with a crucial cooling-off period that would prevent violence. Still other groups, concerned with civil liberties, oppose setting up a program to amass dossiers on the vast majority of law-abiding American citizens. Obviously, there is a range of positions when it comes to waiting periods and background checks for Saturday Night Specials.

At one extreme is the position taken by the Coalition to Stop Gun Violence. "We believe that anything less than a total ban on handgun sales . . . is not going to lead to a meaningful reduction in gun violence," says the Coalition's legislative director, Jeffrey Y. Muchnick. "For the greater good of the community, we will have to pass a ban."

Assault Weapons. Handgun Control takes a similar position when it comes to semiautomatic assault weapons. The organization would ban their sale altogether on the grounds that their primary use is by criminals engaged in street warfare, against each other and against the police. Gun advocates deny this. They say that most assault weapons, even those that are technically handguns, are too large to conceal, that their use in crimes compared to other models is relatively infrequent, and that most of them are owned by law-abiding citizens. In this debate both sides sometimes shift their definition of just what an assault weapon is.

The debate over assault weapons raises larger questions. Should firepower be the determining factor in regulating or banning a specific model of gun? Or should the determining factor be the frequency with which a model (such as the Tec-9 or similar Saturday Night Specials) turns up in crimes?

"To blame the gun for its misuse is to avoid dealing with the real issue," says Ronald E. Stilwell, president of Colt's Manufacturing Co., one of the oldest makers of handguns in America. "The issue is poverty, drugs, jobs," he adds.

Those who would ban specific guns don't automatically disagree with that. But they see excessive firepower and frequent criminal use as overriding factors. The lives at stake come first, they say, and restricting such weapons must take precedence over the long-term remedies. The restrictions they favor run a gamut that includes total bans of certain guns, laws against the manufacture and import of others so that they can be phased out over a period of time, regulation of handgun sales to insure that they don't fall into criminal hands, strong licensing and registration requirements so that all firearms can be tracked if used in a crime, and others.

Questions and Conflicts. Each proposal raises questions, problems, and objections: Should the citizen be licensed, the gun registered, or both? Should guns be registered when they are made or when they are sold? Should resales be regulated, and if so, how?

If a weapon is banned, should there be exceptions for military and police use? For private security firms? For licensed hunting? For *cause*, such as the demonstrable need for self-protection that is a major concern of pro-gun people?

If we ban imports of a specific gun, might not the country of manufacture retaliate by cutting off purchases of American-made guns? What effect would that have on American gun companies and their workers? Should our government take responsibility for the loss of trade?

Is it fair to forbid American manufacturers to make certain guns? Some fear that this could lead to control over other areas of manufacturing. If gun models can be restricted today, they fear, then government can dictate design in whatever field it chooses tomorrow. But they are answered by those who point out that many areas of manufacturing are already subject to government supervision in the public interest. Cars, electrical appliances, drugs, and other products must meet government standards in a variety of areas. Why should not guns be similarly limited in terms of concealability and firepower?

The most serious proposal manufacturers face is one by the Legal Action Project of the Center to Prevent Handgun Violence. It would make the gun company legally responsible for crimes committed with its product. That responsibility would extend to gun dealers who illegally sold handguns to convicted felons, minors, and other high-risk persons.

Should gun dealers be held accountable for their customers? Should sellers be licensed according to standards designed to keep undesirables from joining their ranks? Should their sales be regulated? Should they be forbidden to sell specific types of weapons? How much licensing and

These fully automatic machine guns were assembled from mail-order parts. The ease with which such illegal weapons can be obtained shows the difficulty of enforcing gun-control laws.

regulation is legitimate, and how much constitutes harassment of honest business to an extent that is discriminatory? How much paperwork is justifiable, and how much adds up to an unreasonable burden?

Today the paperwork mainly has to do with registration of gun sales. But regulations vary widely from place to place, and there are many proposals for registration, licensing, and restrictions that would add to it greatly. Should gun buyers as well as gun sellers have to be licensed? If so, should all citizens be eligible for such licenses? If not, just who should be ineligible? Should criminals, alcoholics, and drug addicts be excluded? Minors? People with a history of mental illness?

Increasing numbers of women are insisting on the right to defend themselves with guns. Should battered women be issued gun licenses? Abused children? Teachers in inner-city schools? When is a gun a legitimate defense, and when is it a provocation to violence?

Should the federal government alone be empowered to regulate, license, and register the sale of guns so that laws cannot be circumvented by crossing state or county lines? Or should states and communities be free to regulate themselves on the grounds that conditions are very different, say, in rural Arkansas and metropolitan Boston? Is a combination of federal and local regulation a practical solution?

Behind all these and other sticking points of gun control lie conflicts that often involve basic rights. For instance:

- Restrictions on mail-order sales v. free trade.
- Banning semiautomatic and/or fully automatic rifles v. the freedom to maintain a militia.
- Presumption of innocence v. background checks on gun buyers.

- Keeping track of weapons v. the unreasonable burden of excessive paperwork on the gun merchant.
- Federal regulations v. states' rights.
- Licensing requirements v. the free flow of goods interstate.
- Crime prevention v. prior restraint.

Each of these concerns involves more than just gun regulation. At the same time, each of them affects the position people take on that issue. Because this is so, people are not always consistent about firearms control.

Just how inconsistent they can be is demonstrated by two studies conducted by neutral organizations. The first, a Gallup poll conducted in 1988, indicates that 70 percent of U.S. citizens want stronger gun control laws. The second, a 1989 *Time Magazine*–CNN survey, showed 84 percent believing that Americans have "a right to own guns." Can these two points of view be reconciled?

The answer may lie in another question. Are they really in opposition? Isn't it possible to believe in the Second Amendment "right of the people to keep and bear arms," and at the same time to favor some regulation of guns?

Does Gun Control Work?

Many countries have laws regulating the production, sale, and ownership of firearms nationwide. Forty-one of our country's fifty states have state gun laws. If all federal, state, and local laws pertaining to firearms are added up, the total number of gun laws in the United States comes to over 20,000. Surely so many examples should tell us if gun-control laws work, and should indicate a direction for future legislation.

But it's not quite that simple. Other factors enter into the judgment. Local traditions, cultural differences, density of population, unemployment rates, psychological and sociological influences and pressures, and many other considerations affect the success of a particular gun regulation program.

Gun Control in Britain. Britain, for instance, has had very strong national firearms laws since 1920, and they are vigorously enforced. It is an industrialized nation with a standard of living comparable to that of the United States. It has problems similar to ours in such areas as racial tension, urban poverty, crime, and drugs.

During 1985, 8,092 people were killed by handguns in the United States. Over the same period there were only eight such deaths in Great Britain. Statistics on death by all kinds of firearms, not just handguns, over six years (1983–1989) confirm the wide discrepancy. In the United States, where almost half of all households have guns, the 1990 murder rate was 8.4 per 100,000 people. In Great Britain, where less than 5 percent of households have guns, the rate was 1.97 per 100,000. The rate of suicide by gun was even more telling: 6.8 per 100,000 people in the United States, compared to 0.4 per 100,000 in Britain.

Gun-control advocates credit England's low firearms-related death rate to its gun laws. In Britain, a certificate of permission is required to own any firearm except an antique or an airgun (a BB gun). The certificate, issued by the police, is given only to those who can prove they have a "good reason" to own a gun.

A "good reason" usually involves membership in a hunting or target-shooting club. By law these clubs admit new members only on a six-month trial basis. During that time the applicant must prove his or her genuine interest in sport shooting. If the club finds there is no serious intent, the probationary member is dropped, the certificate is canceled, and the applicant may not own a gun.

Application for both Firearm Certificate and Shot Gun Certificate licenses must be made at local police stations. A neighborhood police officer then calls on the applicant to verify statements made on the application. Usually this officer is acquainted with the applicant. The officer makes sure that the applicant has a secure place to keep a gun and ammunition, a place accessible to neither children nor burglars. If in the police officer's judgment the applicant should for any reason not have a gun, the application may be denied. No explanation need be given.

*British police officers, or "bobbies,"
traditionally do not carry guns.*

Application for the grant, renewal or variation of a Firearm Certificate

Please read the notes on page 4 carefully before completing this form and write in BLOCK CAPITALS except when signing.

Part A Personal details

1 Title (eg Mr, Mrs, Ms)

2 Surname

3 Forename(s)

4 If you have at any time used a name other than those quoted at **2** and **3** above, please give details (including in the case of a married woman, surname before marriage)

5 Date of birth

6 Place of birth

7 Height

8 Nationality

9 Occupation

10 Current home address

Post Code

Telephone number

11 Permanent home address (if different from **10**)

Post Code

Telephone number

12 If you have lived elsewhere than at the addresses quoted at **10** and **11** above during the last five years please give details

Post Code

Telephone number

13 Business address or place of employment

Post Code

Telephone number

14 Have you now or have you ever had:

a Epilepsy? yes [ ] no [ ]

b Any form of mental disorder? yes [ ] no [ ]

If **yes** give details

15 Have you been convicted of any offence?

yes [ ] no [ ]

If **yes** give details

(**Note:** You are not entitled to withhold information about any offence. This includes convictions in places outside Great Britain.)

Part of a four-page application for gun ownership used in Great Britain.

(90)

The applicant must be vouched for by a responsible citizen such as a member of Parliament, a minister, or an established civil servant. This person also may be questioned and investigated. If he (or she) does not measure up, then—once again—the application for a firearm license may be denied without explanation.

A firearm license will not be granted for self-defense. If a licensed weapon is used against a burglar or other malefactor, the gun owner faces charges. The license may be revoked and stiffer penalties may be enforced. Only in the most extraordinary circumstances will such use of the firearm be condoned.

There are stiff penalties for illegal possession of a gun in Great Britain. If an unlicensed weapon is used against a criminal, charges will be brought against the one using it and a jail sentence is likely. Even longtime members of the British National Rifle Association believe that protection is best left to the police. On the other hand, using even a fake gun in a crime may be punished by up to fourteen years in prison.

U.S. supporters of firearms regulation cite British statistics as proof that gun laws work. Most English and Scottish law enforcement officials agree—but not all. One who doesn't is Colin Greenwood, Superintendent of West Yorkshire Police, who, while a fellow at Cambridge University, conducted an in-depth study resulting in his book *Firearms Control: A Study of Armed Crime and Firearms Control in England and Wales*.

Superintendent Greenwood claims that gun licensing has not kept firearms out of the hands of criminals. He points out that when crime began to rise dramatically in England in the 1960s, efforts to enforce anti-pistol laws, and new legislation requiring licensing of rifles and shotguns, were ineffective in halting the increase. He concluded that "the use of firearms in crime was very much less when there were no controls of any sort and when anyone, convicted criminal or lunatic, could buy any type of firearm without restriction. Half a century of strict controls on pistols has ended, perversely, with a far greater use of this class of weapon in crime than ever before."

Other British experts disagree. For example, Dr. Shirley Summerskill, testifying before a committee of Parliament in the late 1970s, cited figures showing that over a twelve-month period there were three hundred times as many robberies involving firearms in the United States as in England. Even given the difference in populations, her figures confirmed for many Britons her closing statement that "it is common knowledge that there is more firearm violence in the United States."

Local Efforts. Law enforcement officials in the United States don't usually argue with that. Many of them have introduced so-called "amnesty programs" to round up illegal guns in their communities. In the spring of 1992, New York City Police Commissioner Lee Brown instituted a month-long program that paid citizens to turn in unregistered guns without penalty. Prices ranged from $25 for a replica dueling pistol to $75 for an AR-15 assault rifle. At the end of the thirty days the city had shelled out $58,375 and collected 1,246 firearms. Commissioner Brown judged this such a success that he extended the program for another month.

Not everyone agreed the program had been successful. Some pointed out that a police precinct in low-crime Staten Island bought 139 weapons, while Manhattan's 34th Precinct, which had 119 murders in 1991, collected only 19 guns. Skeptics said honest citizens were selling guns to the police while criminals were buying them at comparable prices and in far greater numbers on the street.

*New York City Mayor David Dinkins
(right) and Police Commissioner Lee
Brown display a few of the more than
1,200 guns turned in during the first
month of a 1992 amnesty program.*

The program included a ninety-day grace period for assault rifles, giving registered owners of these weapons a chance to get rid of them. The city council had just passed a law making their possession illegal. It was the latest in a body of state and local gun laws affecting New York City.

Despite popular misconceptions, New York City does not lead the nation in crimes of violence. FBI statistics usually rank it about fourteenth, well behind Phoenix, Arizona, and Washington, D. C. The state, however, is a different matter.

With some of the most restrictive state firearms laws in the country, New York state nevertheless ranks first in instances of armed robbery. Florida, which has a permissive state law overriding all local gun ordinances, leans strongly toward guaranteeing the rights of gun owners rather than restricting their firearms. Practically any adult Floridian can buy as many guns of any kind as he or she wants. The FBI rated Florida number one among the states in incidence of violent crimes.

How can that add up? One state with strong gun-control laws and one state comparatively wide open, and yet each leads the nation in a category of gun-related crime. New York law enforcement officials explain it as a result of gun running. Of the 19,000 guns they seized in 1991, more than nine out of ten were purchased legally in states like Florida.

Richard Aborn, former homicide prosecutor and present member of the board of Handgun Control, sees the dilemma of violent cities like New York, Chicago, Houston, and Phoenix as a national one. "This country has never tried national gun control," he points out. "What we have tried is gun control on a state level. But that's like trying to regulate acid rain on a state-by-state basis. We would never do that because acid rain travels freely between states. So do guns."

Pro-gun champions have a different explanation. Florida is a distribution center for the illegal international drug trade, they point out. New York leads the nation as a market for those drugs. With wars between rival distributors and rival street dealers common to both states, naturally they are both prone to violence. But guns are not the cause; drugs are. Win the war against drugs, they argue, and the violence will abate. But until that happens, honest citizens should have the right to arm themselves against the criminals.

Comparisons between Florida and New York, the two states most prone to gun savagery, are muddied by questions of gun runners and out-of-state sales and narcotics smuggling and drug wars. But none of these were significant factors in studies reported in the *New England Journal of Medicine* comparing Seattle, Washington, and Vancouver, British Columbia, in Canada. The two cities are geographically close to one another and alike in size, standard of living, frontier traditions, location, and climate.

The main difference between the two is that Vancouver had strict controls on handguns and concealed weapons while Seattle had a lenient policy toward the sale and carrying of firearms. Seattle had a thirty-day waiting period but otherwise put no obstacles in the way of gun purchases. Vancouver virtually barred all firearms except strictly regulated hunting rifles and made no exceptions in regard to guns for self-defense.

Results of the *Journal of Medicine* comparison are both intriguing and open to interpretation and challenge. The incidence of robberies and burglaries was the same in both cities. Crimes of violence in which firearms played no part also showed no significant difference. However, crimes involving guns occurred at eight times the rate in Seattle as in Vancouver. As might be expected, physical harm to victims was greater in Seattle, and the murder rate was higher.

Gun-control advocates see this study as proof positive that a handgun ban reduces violent crime. On a national level, they predict such a ban would have a significant effect. But Professor Gary Kleck of Florida State University thinks the Seattle-Vancouver study is flawed. He termed the *Journal of Medicine* report "worthless," adding that "there isn't a legitimate gun control expert in the country who regarded it as legitimate research."

There is also disagreement as to the effectiveness of local and state gun-control laws on the books in the United States. One example is the Massachusetts Bartley-Fox Amendment, which has been in effect since 1975. It calls for a compulsory jail term for anyone who carries a firearm without a license.

How well has Bartley-Fox deterred crime? A study by Glenn L. Pierce and William J. Bowers, which appeared in the *Annals of the American Academy of Political and Social Science*, showed that after five years rates of violent crime had decreased. The murder rate fell in Boston alone, as well as in Massachusetts state as a whole.

The NRA disputes these figures. In a 1991 pamphlet, it cited Boston as having risen from "fifth to second most violent among cities over 500,000" in the United States It also claimed that violence had increased 80 percent faster in Massachusetts than in the nation as a whole.

If the statistics seem only to muddy the conclusion, it is perhaps because they involve different criteria and different time periods. "Violence" as a whole may or may not be gun related. Short-term results may be more or less valid than long-term results, depending on whether or not one takes into account changes in the economy, the growth of drug use, racial tensions, and many other factors.

Where pro-gun and pro-control proponents cannot agree on the measuring stick, there is not likely to be agreement on the results of specific laws.

The same applies to New Jersey, which has had strict laws regarding application, waiting period, and licensing since 1971. Handgun Control quotes the New Jersey state police superintendent to the effect that "ten thousand convicted felons have been caught trying to buy handguns" due to the background checks mandated by the law. But pro-gun lobbyists claim that an equal number of legitimate citizens have been prevented from buying guns because the system is deliberately set up to frustrate and discourage them. (In May 1990, New Jersey passed a second law banning assault weapons.)

As in New Jersey, there is disagreement as to how well gun laws have worked in Illinois, Maryland, Pennsylvania, and other states. Even where criteria and time periods are agreed upon, the results are interpreted differently. Advocates are locked into their positions, and there is little willingness to grant any validity to the arguments of the other side.

Fear dictates both positions. But what is the real danger? Is it the gun? Or is it the criminal? What do you think?

8

Youth Has Its Say

We have looked at the many sticking points of gun control. Can they be debated and resolved? Can the larger issues be compromised and settled? Can the pro-gun and anti-gun people find some common ground to settle their differences? Wouldn't the classroom be a good place to begin?

Both as potential victims and as members of society, young people are already concerned with this issue. Can their differing viewpoints offer fresh insights? By way of answer, ten young people, ages fourteen through seventeen, were asked to comment on questions of guns and gun control. Here, in their own words, are their views:

BEN (*He is a fourteen-year-old of varied European-American parentage who attends ninth grade in a small northeastern college community.*): There's definitely a place for guns in society with the police and the military. But I don't know if private citizens should be allowed to have guns.

BUSTER (*Originally from Peru, he is a ninth grader, age fifteen, of Indian, Hispanic, and Chinese heritage. His childhood was rural, but now he lives in the inner city. His name is pronounced* Boo-stair.): Everybody should have a gun; it says it in the Constitution; I can't mess with that.

LIZ (*She is fifteen, in the tenth grade of an urban science-magnet high school, and calls herself a third generation American of Russian extraction.*): But that's why we have the Bill of Rights, to fix the things that we do wrong. We definitely did it wrong because so many people are dying by guns.

BUSTER: You gonna change our right to bear arms?

LIZ: Yes. It's too easy for anybody to walk in off the street and buy a gun. There should be a federal law.

JOSE (*He is a seventeen-year-old Puerto Rican high school dropout from the inner city.*): We like it the way it is. You can't do nothing about it. You can't change the law.

BEN: Those numbers—200 million guns; 35,000 deaths annually—seem really high, especially the suicide rate. If guns weren't available, they'd definitely be a lot lower.

NATASHA (*A suburban sixteen-year-old in the eleventh grade, she is Russian-born.*): But it's not possible to have every single person watched to know if they have a gun. I'd just make much stricter laws on what gets into the country.

ALGERLYNN (*A freshman honor student at a science-magnet high school, she is a fifteen-year-old African-American from the inner city.*) I honestly believe that the government has a lot to do with the guns that come into the country, and the drugs. They hassle the little corner dealers but when we think about it, who is really importing this stuff? I think the government is allowing it.

LIZ: Anyway, the federal government is going about the problem wrong. They're trying to handle this problem through punishment and they're not dealing with prevention.

BEN: A good first step would be to stop manufacturing and selling guns.

NATASHA: I don't think I'd stop that, because of the recession. I don't think that's the answer, that people should lose their jobs.

JOSH (*He is a suburban high-school senior, age seventeen. He defines his heritage as "American-English going back to the Mayflower."*): The Brady Bill would be a start, but politics has it bottled up. All the NRA senators are not going to support it. It was turned down the first time. The NRA likes the fact that they can use an AK-47 to kill a deer. Now what kind of sport is that?

BUSTER: Hey, *amigo*, sometimes a gun is the only way you get something to eat, you know? I don't mean stick up a grocery. I'm saying you get out of the city, you shoot rabbit, squirrel, whatever, maybe that is the only meat you got.

CHARLES (*He is an urban Chinese-American, seventeen years old and in the twelfth grade.*): Hunting is obsolete. You can buy your food at the supermarket. There's no reason to go out there and shoot stag and—

BUSTER: Live in the country, you hunt all the time. Not deer. Stewpot animals. Deer, stag, that's rare.

NATASHA: You should have to show that you have a hunting purpose. Or if you live in a really dangerous neighborhood, there should be a gun test to make sure you have the ability to handle it.

CHARLES: The problem is that people are going to places where they're legal and buying guns in large quantities and

(101)

transporting them across state borders and selling them on the black market.

NATASHA: There should have to be licenses to get those guns.

LIZ: First of all, someone who owns or works in a gun store should be carefully checked out. You don't want a crazy selling guns. Second, when somebody comes to buy a gun, there should be a lot of papers filled out. Everything should be known about the purchaser.

BUSTER: Just forget they got a right to privacy? That's not right.

BEN: If it were really illegal to have a gun, if they could throw you in jail, it wouldn't be as easy to carry a gun around.

CHARLES: They already have strong gun laws in New York. To get a license to carry, you need a very good reason, like transporting a very large amount of money, or you've been threatened. Donald Trump carries a licensed gun because he's rich, so he's at risk. But the normal Joe can't get a license.

MAI (*A Korean-American, she is a sixteen-year-old tenth grader who lives in the suburbs and commutes to private school in the city.*): They should allow people to have guns. If you have gun control, then what about the people that get them illegally and they start shooting people that can't have them?

ALGERLYNN: Oh, yes. I think it's scary how many guns are out on the street. And I think gun control is a good idea, but the reality is that people are out there with danger around them at all times. If having a gun is going to prevent you from getting into a problem, then maybe it's okay.

JOSH: America is insecure. Why do all these homes have guns? They want to feel that if an intruder came into the house they can defend themselves. It used to be I'll get an attack dog or locks or alarms to insure my safety. Now it's come to the point where guns are it. Society sees guns as the only answer.

BUSTER: Storekeepers gotta have guns to defend themselves. If you don't sell guns, store owners gonna die. Thieves, they're gonna come and shoot them.

ALGERLYNN: I don't think using guns is a very good thing to do, but in our society it's not practical to restrict the use of guns.

BUSTER: All the teenagers who already got guns, they're not gonna get rid of them just because America, she says you can't have them.

LIZ: We can't completely eliminate guns because people are very scared now; people feel they have to defend themselves, and that's a terrible thing.

BEN: The issue of security is valid. But it should be made to work so that the police can protect the civilians. People shouldn't feel the need to protect themselves.

LIZ: That is the purpose of the government—for our protection.

ALGERLYNN: There was a time when my cousin wanted to give me a gun to go to school through a tough neighborhood. He thought it would be better if I was packing. But I didn't feel comfortable about carrying a gun. So I didn't.

JOSE: You can't take guns away. We can't live without guns. We gonna get killed without guns. Everybody got beef and you ain't got a pistol, you're gonna get shot. If I don't got a pistol, then somebody with a pistol's gonna shoot me. They got no respect for anybody, that's the truth.

MAI: If I moved to a dangerous neighborhood, or was traveling late at night, I'd get a gun.

MAYA (*Silent until now, she is seventeen and in the eleventh grade. Her background is Middle Eastern.*): I have friends who have guns. They have lots of beef with people and they need to have protection.

LIZ: Gangs are the biggest problem. Someone's in a fight, they call out twenty guys and say come in with guns. Where do they get the guns? Connections. A kid has an older brother who knows someone in a gang who knows a drug dealer who has easy access to guns.

JOSE: Easy to buy a gun. You give me two hundred fifty dollars, you get a pistol like that.

BUSTER: Fifty bucks even. It depends what gun you get.

CHARLES: For fifty you'll get a gun with like six to eight dead bodies on it. Get caught with it, you could face all those charges. A gun used in a crime—that lowers the price.

BEN: Gee, what a sheltered life I live. The only person I've ever seen with a gun is a cop. I've never known of any of my friends carrying guns. I've never heard about guns being used on any of my friends, or on anyone in my school. Where I live, you aren't afraid when you go to school. If you see a cop and you're carrying a gun you're in big trouble.

JOSE: Cops! They're selling the guns with the hits on them. Take them from the criminals, sell them cheap to the kids 'cause they're hot, then arrest the kids. Those the fifty-dollar guns Buster's talking about.

BUSTER: I never heard of that.

LIZ: Maybe they should take away the cops' guns like in England and Ireland.

MAYA: The police need to use guns to protect themselves. If the drug dealers have guns, then the police should be equally armed.

JOSH: It's gotten to the point here where the cops are outgunned. The cop with a little eight-shooter, or a six-shooter, and then you have the drug dealer on the corner with his machine gun arsenal.

LIZ: I'm not sure that the police are used as efficiently and productively as possible. I think maybe there needs to be better training. They're not focusing as much as they could on the serious problems.

CHARLES: You get all through cop-bashing and you'll have no choice but to buy a gun—and to use it.

LIZ: I don't think I could ever do that.

BUSTER: Not everybody packs means to use the gun. Guy likes to flash a gun to show off to his friends, show them that he has a gun and you know, he'll get popular like that. Guys will go like, "Oh, you have a gun; that's cool." But sometimes they say like let's go up to this party and if they get into trouble, they start shooting. I think it's stupid.

ALGERLYNN: I do think that most of the people who pack intend to use. If you are carrying a gun to defend yourself, then you must be thinking that you're going to shoot some-body.

MAYA: Usually people have guns because they know the other person has a gun and you can't protect yourself with fists against someone who has a gun. Two wrongs don't make a right, but—you have to defend yourself.

MAI: If I had a gun and some big guy threatened robbery, I'd fire it up in the air. If the guy wouldn't back off, I would shoot him.

ALGERLYNN: So now he's dead.

MAI: Oh, he can't die like that. I would call an ambulance.

ALGERLYNN: So he's paralyzed for life, whatever. All because of the lousy couple of dollars in your pocketbook. How you gonna feel?

MAI: I feel bad about shooting him and possibly killing him, but it's not his right in the first place to violate me. I have rights too.

ALGERLYNN: I don't think that shooting somebody that says give me your money is okay.

CHARLES: The issue isn't whether I give him my money or I'm gonna shoot him. The issue is whether I give him my money or I get shot. He's threatening your life for X amount of money. If a person takes away your rights to life, he loses his own rights.

BEN: I don't know. If I had a gun, I guess I'd pull it out, but I don't know if I'd use it.

MAYA: Then you're trapped.

BEN: I guess I could shoot him in the foot.

JOSH: But you're nervous. Your hand's shaking. You could hit him anywhere. Besides, I read how most handguns use soft ammunition and it fragments. You could hit him in the foot and maybe sever an artery and kill him anyway.

BEN: Hell! What do I do? Good God! I'm probably going to hand it over.

JOSE: Oh, you really smart, man. Now the crook, he has your gun; who can he kill?

BEN: All right, so I blew it. I shouldn't have been carrying the gun in the first place.

JOSE: You should have used it.

BEN: Then a different person's dead.

BUSTER: Maybe better him than you. It's not like you got the time for all this. You're under pressure.

ALGERLYNN: I've been taught conflict resolution, and what goes through your head in a pressure situation like that is not a very good thing to do. I don't think that "no time to think" is a good excuse. You have to be thinking all the time. If stopping to think is a check, that's good.

JOSE: That's a crock! If they insane, I'm gonna put a bullet in their head. That's my style. And I ain't goin' to jail.

BUSTER: Man, you are watching too much TV.

MAI: Television does have an influence. I think if they didn't watch violence so much, people wouldn't be so violent.

JOSH: It plays into a whole macho image. To be a man you have to have a gun; you have to prove that you're the toughest guy around.

MAYA: If I want violence I'll just go out in the streets; I don't need to watch television.

ALGERLYNN: That's because people have no respect for life anymore. It's so easy to take life and so the only life that somebody will respect is maybe their own, or maybe their kid's, their family's.

JOSE: Sure. Your own gotta come first. I got the gun, I'm gonna shoot first.

ALGERLYNN: But the person you're about to shoot may be robbing because their kid is starving. I don't think that money is worth life.

CHARLES: You're really saying defending yourself is not a reason to use a gun. I don't buy that. Somebody is threatening my life, I defend my life by taking his life. That's what the gun was designed for.

JOSH: You have to agree with the NRA that guns don't just walk out and kill people. Even so, killing someone's made so much easier by a gun. That's what it's about. Guns don't kill people, but they are a means for everyone to kill.

CHARLES: Just the fact that people have guns kind of controls itself. If one moron has a gun and another moron has a gun and the first moron is so high on his macho-ism that he's ready to put his neck out, then he might as well be dead. There's two less morons with guns to deal with.

MAYA: Suppose one moron shoots me accidentally?

CHARLES: That happens all the time.

JOSH: You're more likely to kill someone in your own family than you are to kill an intruder with a gun.

CHARLES: To defeat this gun problem, we have to defeat macho-ism.

JOSH: Not easy. Guns are an addiction. The power to take away lives makes people feel powerful, like God. If you have a gun, you can do anything. If someone is messing with you and you don't like them, you can shoot them. That's power in this world, to be able to kill someone.

MAI: I think all the gun problems start with drug problems. They need the money so they rob people with the guns in order to get more drugs, and the cycle goes on and on. What do you do?

MAYA: Get a gun, I guess. You have to fight fire with fire.

BEN: If you fight fire with fire, everything will burn down.

A Last
Word

It is not surprising that these young people could not resolve the question of gun control. The adult leadership of this country has been struggling with it for many years without arriving at a resolution. There are no easy answers, and the questions will be with us for many years to come.

Still, they must be addressed. The mounting death toll from firearms will not allow them to be ignored. Young people make up a significant part of that death toll. It follows that they must focus on the problem early and that their voices must be heard.

Silence, it has been said, can be the greatest crime of all. No matter which side of the gun-control question you are on, it is your duty to make your voice heard. If decision-making is an obligation adults owe to their children, then it is also true that it will one day be your obligation to your children.

Consider the problems of guns and gun control. Discuss and debate them. Arrive at your convictions, and then stand by them. Ultimately, the resolution will be in your hands.

That is perhaps the most hopeful prospect of all.

Ted Gottfried
New York City

Notes

Introduction
"Our nation is armed to the teeth . . ." *Congressional Quarterly's Editorial Research Reports,* Nov. 13, 1987, p. 596.

"It's a nasty truth . . ." Ibid.

Chapter Two
"the Court plainly recognized . . ." Richard Gardiner, *Vigilance in Behalf of Liberty: The Second Amendment in its 200th Year* (Washington, D.C., National Rifle Association, 1991), flyer essay.

Chapter Three
"An eye for an eye." *Houston Chronicle,* March 18, 1992, p. 12.

"That way all of our young people . . ." Author's interview with youth counselor, Amherst, Mass., March 25, 1992.

Each year some 1,500 Americans . . . *NRA Firearms Fact Card 1992* (Washington, D.C., NRA Institute for Legislative Action).

Between 11,000 and 12,000 more . . . *Handgun Facts* (Washington, D.C., Center to Prevent Handgun Violence, 1991), flyer. Also

Twelve Tall Tales (Washington, D.C., NRA Institute for Legislative Action, May 1991), pamphlet.

Among these suicides . . . *Teen Suicide & Handguns* (Washington, D.C., Center to Prevent Handgun Violence, April 1989), flyer. (Quoting from Centers for Disease Control report, *Youth Suicide Surveillance, 1986.*)

"Children are exposed . . ." *New York Times*, March 30, 1992, Op Ed piece by James Brady.

"Suicidal teenagers who have been drinking . . ." *Teen Suicide & Handguns*. (Quoting from study cited in text.)

"Hey kid, if you really want to kill yourself . . ." Author's personal files.

In one small Arizona town . . . Author's interviews with Cottonwood, Arizona, hospital personnel who treated victim.

Chapter Four
As part of a three-year study . . . *It Can Happen to You* (Washington, D.C., National Rifle Association, July 1991), pamphlet. (Quoting from Justice Department study conducted by criminologist James Wright of the University of Massachusetts.)

"in self defense . . ." *A Question of Self Defense* (Washington, D.C., NRA Institute for Legislative Action, October 1991), pamphlet.

"50 percent drop in fatal mishaps . . ." *Twelve Tall Tales*.

On February 16 . . . *New York Times*, May 10, 1992, p. B-27.

"I enjoy it, just going out . . ." *New York Times*, March 9, 1992, p. A-1.

Chapter Five
A burglar broke into the home . . . *The Armed Citizen* (Washington, D.C., National Rifle Association, 1989), p. 193.

Shortly after a record stock-market plunge . . . *Congressional Quarterly's Editorial Research Reports*, Nov. 13, 1987, p. 590–91.

"These guns are not wearing out . . ." *New York Times,* March 8, 1992, pp. 1 and 30.

The Tec-9 is the weapon of preference . . . *New York Times,* March 10, 1992, p. A-18.

"they are designed . . ." *New York Times,* March 10, 1992, p. A-1.

"This gun is primarily . . ." *New York Times,* March 10, 1992, p. A-18.

"You can fill it . . ." Ibid.

Chapter Six

"We may not . . ." Author's interview with commander, Central Police Station, Dundee, Scotland, April 1992.

"Officers must set . . ." Author's interview with police officer, Dublin, Ireland, April 1992.

"We view the primary reason . . ." *New York Times,* March 12, 1992, p. D-21.

"We believe that anything less . . ." *New York Times,* April 3, 1992, p. A-15.

"To blame the gun for its misuse . . ." *New York Times,* March 8, 1992, p. 30.

Chapter Seven

"The 1990 murder rate . . ." Statistics are from the *World Health Statistics Annual* and *International Crime Statistics,* as cited by Michael Wolff in *Where We Stand: Can America Make It in the Global Race for Wealth, Health and Happiness* (New York: Bantam Books, 1992), and from *The New York Times* (April 4, 1992).

"it is common knowledge . . ." Kates, Don B., Jr. (Ed.), *Restricting Handguns: The Liberal Skeptics Speak Out* (North River Press, Inc., 1979), p. 34–35.

"This country has never tried . . ." Author's interview with Richard Aborn, New York City, March 1992.

"worthless . . . there isn't a legitimate . . ." *Twelve Tall Tales.*

Chronology: Legislation and Court Decisions

1689   English Bill of Rights establishes prerogative of private citizens to bear arms.

1777   British Colonial Office attempts unsuccessfully to deprive colonial Americans of the right to own guns.

1791   The Bill of Rights is added to the United States Constitution. Its ambiguously worded Second Amendment says the people's right to "bear arms shall not be infringed."

1846   Georgia state courts strike down a law prohibiting dueling pistols on the grounds that it is in violation of the Second Amendment.

1876   In *United States* v. *Cruikshank,* the U.S. Supreme Court finds that the Constitution does not bestow an unconditional right to bear arms.

1886   The Supreme Court, in *Presser* v. *Illinois,* straddles the fence on the question of citizens constituting themselves an armed militia.

1927   A federal law is passed prohibiting shipping "concealable" firearms through the mail.

1934   The National Firearms Act restricts sales and ownership of machine guns.

1939   The right of local communities to limit sales of shotguns with barrels less than 18 inches (46 centimeters) long is confirmed by the Supreme Court in *United States* v. *Miller* because such a weapon would not be suitable for militia use.

1968   The Federal Gun Control Act is passed. It forbids crossing a state line to buy or sell a handgun, and mandates record-keeping by gun sellers.

1975   The State of Massachusetts enacts the Bartley-Fox Amendment making jail compulsory for anyone carrying a firearm without a license.

1986   The Firearms Owners' Protection Act and subsequent amendments weakening the Federal Gun Control Act are signed into law. The combined effect nullifies or weakens many state and local laws involving interstate transport of firearms.

1989   President George Bush signs a Congressional bill banning the import of assault weapons like the Soviet made AK-47 used in a California schoolyard massacre.

1990   New Jersey bans assault weapons.

1991   A bill to ban sales of American-made semiautomatic weapons is defeated in Congress.
        The Brady Bill, requiring a waiting period before the buyer can take possession of a handgun, is tacked on to a highly controversial anticrime bill.

1992   At the end of the legislative session, the Brady Bill, which at different times President Bush has said he will and won't sign, is still stalled in the Senate.

For Further
Information

Bode, Janet. *Beating the Odds: Stories of Unexpected Achievers.* (Drawings by Stan Mack.) New York: Franklin Watts, 1991.

Freedman, Warren. *The Privilege to Keep and Bear Arms: The Second Amendment and Its Interpretation.* Westport, Conn.: Quorum Books, 1989.

Hawkes, Nigel. *Gun Control.* New York: Gloucester Press/Watts, 1988.

Landau, Elaine. *Armed America: The Status of Gun Control.* Englewood Cliffs, N.J.: Julian Messner, 1991.

Landau, Elaine. *Teenage Violence.* Englewood Cliffs, N.J.: Julian Messner, 1990.

Roberts, Joseph B., Jr. (Ed.). *The Armed Citizen.* Washington, D.C.: The National Rifle Association of America, 1989.

Silberman, Charles E. *Criminal Violence, Criminal Justice.* New York: Random House, 1978.

Wright, James D., and Peter H. Rossi. *Armed and Considered Dangerous: A Survey of Felons and Their Firearms.* Hawthorne, N.Y.: Aldine De Gruyter, 1986.

Organizations to Contact

American Society of Criminology, 1314 Kinnear Road, Suite 212, Columbus, Ohio 43212

Center to Prevent Handgun Violence, 1225 Eye Street, NW, Suite 1100, Washington, DC 20005

Citizens Action for a Safer Harlem, 356 West 123 Street, New York, NY 10027

Firearms Research and Identification Association, 1608 Nogales St., Suite 360, Rowland Heights, CA 91748

Handgun Control Inc., 1400 K Street, NW, Washington, DC 20005

Independence Institute, 14142 Denver West Parkway #101, Golden, CO 80401

Parents of Murdered Children of New York State, Inc., 26 West 84th Street, New York, NY 10024

Research and Information Division, NRA Institute for Legislative Action, 1600 Rhode Island Avenue, NW, Washington, DC 20036

Second Amendment Foundation, James Madison Building, 12500 NE 10th Place, Bellevue, WA 98005

Index

Page numbers in *italics* refer to illustrations.

Gun safety, 22, 51, 53

Handgun Control, Inc., 17n, 42, 65, 66, 78, 81–82, 97
Handguns, types of, 60, 62
Highland Park, Michigan, 50
Hijackings, 65
Hinckley, John W., Jr., 79
Hunting, 13, 28, 34, 45–46, 55, 56, 57–58, 70, 72, 88, 101

Illinois, 34, 37, 41–42, 69, 97
Inner cities, 41
Innocent victims, 37, 42–44, 46, 62
Instant checks, 79, 81
Interstate transport of guns, 66, 77, 94–95
Intratec Tec-9 semiautomatic pistol, 67, 68, 69, 82
Ireland, Republic of, 75, 76

Jealousy, 46
Jennings, James, 57
Jensen, Robert E., 57
Justice, Department of, 47, 48

Kane, Arthur, 59–60
Kennedy, Edward M., 14
Kennedy, John F., 14, 72
Kennedy, Robert F., 14
Kennesaw, Georgia, 34
King, Martin Luther, Jr., 72
Kleck, Gary, 48, 96

League of Women Voters, 42
Legal Action Project of the Center to Prevent Handgun Violence, 83

Licensing, 82, 83, 85, 86, 91, 97, 102
Local efforts, 92, 93, 94–97
Long guns, 69–70
Los Angeles riots (1992), 14, 16, 76

Machine guns, 67, 77, 84
Madison, James, 27
Mail-order sales, 77, 84, 85
Martin, LeRoy, 69
Maryland, 97
Masculine firearms culture, 46
Massachusetts Bartley-Fox Amendment, 96
McCann, Kenneth, 67
McClure-Volkmer Amendments, 78
Metal bullets, 64–65
Metal detectors, 38, 65
Michigan, 50
Minutemen, 26
Montgomery, Alabama, 50
Morton Grove, Illinois, 34
Muchnick, Jeffrey Y., 81
Murders, 13, 38, 41, 45, 53, 65, 88

National Center for Health Statistics, 13
National Education Association, 42
National Firearms Act of 1934, 77
National League of Cities, 42
National Rifle Association (NRA), 14, 17n, 48, 49, 50, 51, 53, 54, 64, 66, 72, 74, 79, 81, 96, 101, 108